Y0-CAD-765

10 Minute Guide to
Excel for Windows™

Michael L. Miller

A Division of Macmillan Computer Publishing

11711 North College, Carmel, Indiana 46032 USA

International Standard Book Number: 0-672-30222-5
Library of Congress Catalog Card Number: 91-61594

Acquisitions Editor: *Mary-Terese E. Cozzola Cagnina*
Manuscript Editor: *Ronda Carter Henry*
Cover Design: *Dan Armstrong*
Book Design: *Dan Armstrong, reVisions Plus, Inc.*
Production Assistance: *Claudia Bell, Bob LaRoche, Sarah Leatherman, Howard Peirce, Mary Beth Wakefield*
Indexer: *Hilary J. Adams*
Technical Reviewer: *Tracy Kaufman*

Printed in the United States of America

Trademarks

Contents

Introduction

Perhaps you walked into work this morning and found Excel for Windows installed on your computer. There is also a note stuck to your monitor: "We need a budget prepared for an upcoming meeting." Now what?

A few things are certain:

• You need a method of finding your way around Excel quickly and easily.

• You need to identify and learn the tasks necessary to accompish your particular goals.

• You need a clear-cut, plain-English guide to learn about the basic features of the program.

Welcome to the *10 Minute Guide to Excel for Windows*.

Because you don't have the luxury of sitting down uninterrupted for hours at a time to learn Excel, this *10 Minute Guide* teaches lessons that can be completed in 10 minutes or less. Since you are presented information in bite-sized, self-contained modules, you can stop and start as often as you like. Now you can learn exactly what you need, at your own pace—and in 10 minutes or less!

What is the 10 Minute Guide?

The *10 Minute Guide* is a new approach to learning computer programs. Instead of trying to teach you *everything* about a particular software product (and ending up with an 800-page book in the process), the *10 Minute Guide* teaches you only the most often-used features, using a series of short, focused lessons.

The *10 Minute Guide* teaches you about programs without relying on technical jargon. With straightforward, easy-to-follow explanations and special artwork, called *icons*, to call your attention to important tips and definitions, the *10 Minute Guide* makes learning a new software program quick and easy.

The following icons help you find your way around in the *10 Minute Guide to Excel for Windows:*

 Timesaver Tip icons offer shortcuts and hints for using the program effectively.

 Plain English icons define new terms.

 Panic Button icons appear where new users often run into trouble.

In addition, a list of Excel functions is included at the end of the book, providing you with a quick guide to Excel features that are not given full coverage in this book.

Specific conventions are used to help you find your way around Excel as easily as possible:

What you type	Within numbered steps, the information you type is printed in a second color.
Menu names	The names of menus, commands, buttons, and dialog boxes are shown with the first letter capitalized for easy recognition.

In addition, this book assumes you are familiar with Windows and Windows operating conventions. It is assumed that you will be operating Excel with a mouse, although most instructions can also be implemented with the keyboard. If you are not familiar with Windows operations, refer to the DOS and Windows Primer in the back of this book.

The *10 Minute Guide to Excel for Windows* is organized in 26 lessons, ranging from basic startup to more advanced operations. Remember, however, that nothing in this book is *difficult.* All lessons can be completed in 10 minutes or less.

Who Should Use the *10 Minute Guide to Excel for Windows?*

The *10 Minute Guide to Excel for Windows* is for anyone who:

- Needs to learn Excel quickly.

- Wants a clear, concise guide to the most important features of Excel.

- Is switching to Excel from another program and needs a quick guide to the essential program features.

What is Excel?

Excel is an advanced spreadsheet designed specifically for the Windows operating environment. Using a familiar row-and-column format, Excel allows you to manipulate numeric data in a variety of ways. Instead of using ledger paper, calculator, and pencil, you can now use Excel to do both simple and complex number-crunching activities.

In addition, Excel offers sophisticated charting capabilities that enable you to express your data graphically. Excel has always been known for producing presentation-quality output, and now Excel 3 adds the ability to combine charts and numeric data on a single worksheet. Windows' graphics and Excel 3's new Tool Bar feature make Excel one of the easiest spreadsheets to use.

For Further Reference...

SAMS publishes several other books that will help increase your productivity with Excel after you've completed this *10 Minute Guide:*

The First Book of Excel for Windows

Excel for Windows Bible

10 Minute Guide to Windows 3

Lesson 1
Starting and Exiting Excel for Windows

In this lesson you'll learn how to start and end a typical Excel work session.

Starting Excel

To properly use Excel, you need to master a handful of essential Windows operations, including opening, selecting, maximizing, dragging, and scrolling. If these terms are unfamiliar to you, or if you need an overview of basic keyboard and mouse operations in Windows, see the DOS and Windows Primer in the back of this book.

Pull-down menu In Windows, the menu bar is comprised of several *pull-down menus*. A pull-down menu is a menu that remains *hidden* in a menu bar until you use the mouse or the keyboard to open or *pull down* the complete menu. The complete menu contains additional options; after the main menu is pulled down, you may then *select* any of these additional options. Almost all Excel and Windows operations are accessed via pull-down menus.

1

Starting Excel is similar to starting any Windows application. To start Excel you must be running Windows. From within Windows, follow these steps:

1. Maximize the Program Manager.

2. From within the Program Manager, open the program group that holds the Excel icon (see Figure 1-1).

3. Select the Microsoft Excel icon.

4. Double-click on the icon or press Enter.

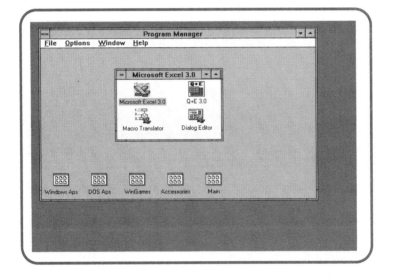

Figure 1-1. *The Program Manager with the Excel program group open.*

The Excel opening screen appears (see Figure 1-2) with a blank worksheet titled *Sheet 1* on-screen. Excel is now ready for you to use.

Worksheet A worksheet is a file divided into cells; each individual cell represents the intersection of a row and a column.

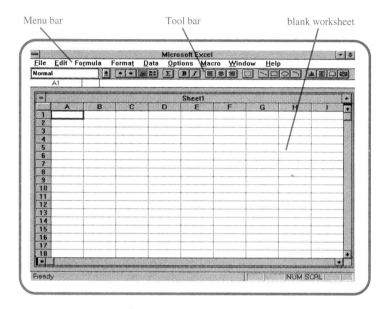

Figure 1-2. The opening screen.

All Excel operations are initiated from the Menu bar and the Tool bar, located at the top of the screen. Each operation will be explained in later lessons.

Exiting Excel

To exit Excel and return to Windows, follow these steps:

1. Pull down the File menu.

2. Select the Exit option (see Figure 1-3).

3

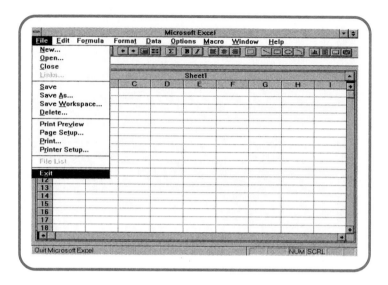

Figure 1-3. *Exiting Excel.*

If you have unsaved files open, Excel will prompt you to save them. Excel will then close itself and return you to the main Windows screen.

In this lesson you learned how to enter and exit Excel. In the next lesson you will learn about the Excel worksheet window.

Lesson 2
Navigating the Excel Worksheet Window

In this lesson you'll learn how to move around the Excel window.

Introducing the Excel Worksheet Window

The Excel screen is similar to that of many Windows applications, which is one of the benefits of working in the Windows environment. If you know how to use one Windows application, it is easy to get up and running quickly with other Windows programs.

Table 2-1 explains each of the main elements of the Excel worksheet window. Refer to Figure 2-1 to see the location of each item in the window. Later lessons will show you how to use these elements to perform specific tasks.

Table 2-1. Elements of the Worksheet Window.

Item	Function
Title bar	Displays the name of the current worksheet
Menu bar	Displays the names of the pull-down menus
Formula bar	Displays the data in the active cell
Tool bar	Displays a series of buttons that automate common Excel tasks
Reference area	Displays the name of the active cell
Control menu button	Clicking on this button pulls down the Control menu; double-clicking on this button closes the current worksheet or program
Minimize button	Reduces the current window to an icon
Maximize button	Enlarges the current window to full-screen
Scroll bars	Enable you to move through the worksheet either vertically or horizontally
Row heading	Identifies the numbered rows of cells
Column heading	Identifies the lettered columns of cells

Item	Function
Status bar	Displays information about the last command selected and the state of the worksheet window
Active cell	This is the cell currently selected (it is surrounded by a heavy border)
Mouse pointer	Displays the location of the mouse on-screen

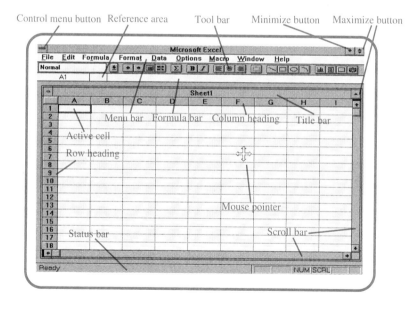

Figure 2-1. *The Worksheet Window.*

Moving with the Mouse

To initiate most Excel commands with the mouse, you simply *point and click.* You can do this by moving the mouse pointer to a Menu name or button in the window and clicking the left mouse button.

The point and click method works best when navigating around the worksheet or using the Tool bar. It is slightly more complex when using pull-down menus.

To access the pull-down menus in the Menu bar with the mouse, follow these steps:

1. Move the mouse pointer to the menu.

2. Click the left mouse button to pull down the menu.

3. Move the mouse pointer to the menu option.

4. Click the left mouse button to select the menu option or click outside the pull-down menu to close it.

Maximizing and Minimizing

As with all Windows programs, you can change the size of the window by clicking on the side or corner of it with the mouse, and dragging the window until it reaches the desired size. To increase the window to full-screen or shrink it to an icon, simply click on the Maximize or Minimize button.

Sensible Sizing Unless you are exchanging data between Excel and another Windows program, it is easier to work with Excel in full-screen mode.

Using the Keyboard

While it is best to use a mouse with Excel, most operations can also be performed with keyboard commands. You can use the cursor keys to move from cell to cell in the worksheet, and you can access the Menu bar by using the function keys.

Table 2-2 details the key combinations that enable you to move around the worksheet.

Key Combinations When two keys are pressed simultaneously to initiate some operation, they are shown as two key names with a plus (+) sign in between. For example, Ctrl+End represents a key combination in which you would press the Ctrl key and the End key simultaneously to execute the action. Remember, you only press the keys, not the plus sign in between.

Table 2-2. Worksheet Movement Keys.

Key	Function
↑	Move up one cell
↓	Move down one cell
→	Move right one cell
←	Move left one cell
Tab	Move right one cell
Shift+Tab	Move left one cell
Ctrl+Home	Move to cell A1
PgUp	Move one screen up
PgDn	Move one screen down

(continued)

Table 2-2. (continued)

Key	Function
Ctrl+PgUp	Move one screen left
Ctrl+PgDn	Move one screen right
End	Move to the right-most column (you must have data in the right-most column to move to it)
Ctrl+End	Move to the last cell in the worksheet

To access the pull-down menus in the Menu bar with the keyboard, follow these steps:

1. Press F10. This activates the Menu bar with the File menu highlighted (as shown in Figure 2-2).

2. Use the right and left arrow keys to move to the menu.

3. Press Enter to pull down the menu.

4. Use the up and down arrow keys to move to the menu option.

5. Press Enter to select the menu option, or press Alt or Esc to close the menu.

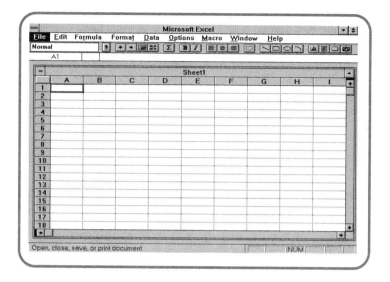

Figure 2-2. *The File menu highlighted in the Menu bar.*

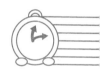

Selecting Menus Quickly If you're using the keyboard, you can select a menu by pressing Alt and the underlined letter of the menu name.

There are numerous other keyboard shortcuts to initiate Excel commands. See the inside back cover of this book for a full list of these shortcuts.

In this lesson you learned how to move around the Excel worksheet window with both the keyboard and the mouse. In the next lesson you will learn more about the Excel Tool bar and menus and dialog boxes.

11

Lesson 3

Using Excel Menus and the Tool Bar

In this lesson you'll learn how to use the Excel menu system and the new Tool bar feature.

All Excel commands can be invoked from the menu system. The Menu bar contains the main pull-down menus, which are used to access various submenus. From these submenus, you can access dialog boxes that contain numerous commands and options. In addition, common Excel commands can be implemented from the Tool bar. This lesson leads you through Excel's main menus, dialog boxes, and the Tool bar.

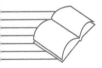

Dialog box A dialog box is a box that appears on-screen after you select certain menu options or commands. Dialog boxes can request additional information, alert you to incorrectly typed information, and provide you with information on your current operation.

Excel's Main Menu System

Excel's main Menu bar contains nine menus (see Figure 3-1), each with numerous options and submenus.

File   Accesses various file-oriented commands, including those for opening, closing, saving, and printing worksheets

Edit   Accesses various editing commands, including copy, cut, and paste

Formula   Accesses commands that let you create formulas in your worksheet

Format   Accesses submenus that let you change the appearance and format of your worksheet and its data

Data   Accesses commands specific to Excel's database functions, including the Sort command

Options   Accesses special commands for printing, displaying, and customizing the worksheet and work environment

Macro   Accesses commands for creating and running macros

Window   Accesses commands that let you work with multiple worksheets in multiple windows on-screen

Help   Accesses the on-line help system

Main Menu bar

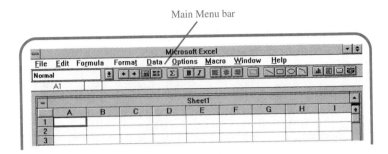

Figure 3-1. *The main Menu bar.*

There are other menu bars that appear when you are performing nonworksheet tasks. You will see alternate menu bars when working with charts and info sheets, for example. These alternate menu bars operate similarly to the main Menu bar, but with menus and options specialized for these alternate tasks.

Follow these steps to select an item from one of the main menus:

1. Pull down a menu from the Menu bar.

2. Select a menu option from the pull-down menu (see Figure 3-2).

3. If a dialog box appears, select an option.

Note that you can select either *long menus* or *short menus* in Excel. To change this option follow these steps:

1. Pull down the Options menu.

2. Select either the Short Menus or Long Menus option from the pull-down menu.

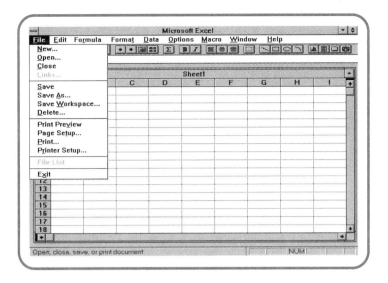

Figure 3-2. *The Menu bar with the File menu pulled down.*

Long Menus Even though the number of options might seem overwhelming at first, you have more control over Excel if you select the *Long Menus* option.

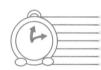

Excel's Tool Bar

Situated at the top of the screen for easy mouse access, the Tool bar (see Figure 3-3) contains those Excel commands that you'll use the most. Each command is activated by a *button;* pressing each button is like activating an on/off switch for that operation.

15

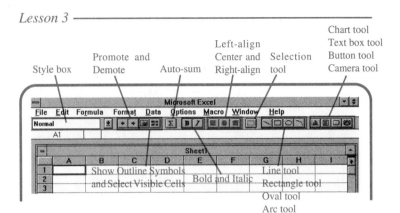

Figure 3-3. *The Tool bar.*

The Tool bar contains these options:

Style box	Defines and applies styles to a cell or group of cells
Promote and demote	Promotes (moves selected columns/rows up a level) and demotes (moves selected columns/rows down a level) sections of your worksheet when in the outline mode
Show outline symbols	Turns outline mode on or off
Select visible cells	Selects all visible cells in your worksheet when in outline mode
Auto-sum	Automatically sums a column or row of numbers
Bold	Applies bold formatting to a cell or group of cells
Italic	Applies italic formatting to a cell or group of cells

Left-align	Left-aligns all text in a selection
Center	Centers all text in a selection
Right-align	Right-aligns all text in a selection
Selection tool	Selects graphic objects you want to move, size, or format
Line tool	Draws a line on your worksheet
Rectangle tool	Draws a rectangle on your worksheet
Oval tool	Draws an oval on your worksheet
Arc tool	Draws an arc on your worksheet
Chart tool	Creates a chart from the data selected in your worksheet
Text box tool	Creates a text box on your worksheet
Button tool	Creates a button on your worksheet that can be linked to a macro
Camera tool	Takes a *picture* of a selected area of your worksheet for copy and paste purposes

Most of the Tool bar buttons operate in a similar fashion:

1. Select a cell or range of cells in your worksheet.

2. Click on a button from the Tool bar.

Selecting a range of cells To select a range of cells with your mouse, simply hold down the left mouse button and drag the mouse pointer across the area. To select a range of cells with the keyboard, hold down the Shift key while you use the arrow keys to move from cell to cell.

In this lesson you learned about the Menu bar and the Tool bar. In the next lesson you will learn how to open and save Excel worksheets.

Lesson 4
Creating, Opening, and Saving Excel Worksheets

In this lesson you'll learn how to create and save new worksheets, and open and save existing worksheets.

Creating a New Excel Worksheet

Follow these steps to create a new Excel worksheet:

1. Pull down the File menu.

2. Select the New option.

3. A dialog box (see Figure 4-1) appears, prompting you to select the kind of file you want to open. Select the Worksheet option.

4. Select OK to close the dialog box.

You now have a new blank worksheet on your screen (If the Sheet1 worksheet was already on-screen, this new sheet will be called *Sheet2*). You can now enter data into this blank worksheet.

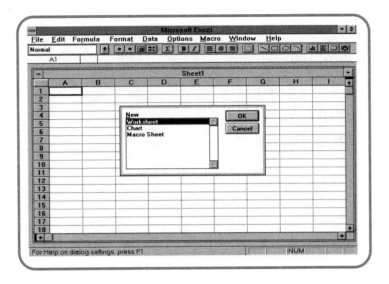

Figure 4-1. *Opening a new worksheet.*

Saving a New Excel Worksheet

When you are finished with a worksheet, you need to save it to a disk. Saving a new worksheet is slightly different from saving an existing worksheet. In the case of saving a new worksheet, you must first give the worksheet a name.

To save a new worksheet, follow these steps:

1. Pull down the File menu.

2. Select the Save As option.

3. When the dialog box appears (see Figure 4-2), delete SHEET2.XLS and type a new name, with no more than eight characters, such as **10MIN01.** Excel will automatically apply the .XLS file extension.

4. Select OK to close the dialog box.

Figure 4-2. Saving a new worksheet.

You can save a worksheet in file formats other than the standard Excel format by clicking on the Options button in the dialog box.

Saving to a different directory Excel will automatically save your worksheet into the default Excel directory. You can specify a different directory by typing the full directory name into the dialog box, such as **C:\DATA\EXCELDOC\10MIN01.XLS.**

Opening an Existing Excel Worksheet

You will often want to open a worksheet that you created during a previous session. To open an existing worksheet, follow these steps:

1. Pull down the File menu.

2. Select the Open option.

3. When the dialog box appears (see Figure 4-3), select the file you wish to open from the File list on the left of the dialog box. If the file is not in the current directory, select a different directory from the Directories list on the right of the dialog box. For this example, select the 10MIN01.XLS file from the list.

4. Select OK to close the dialog box.

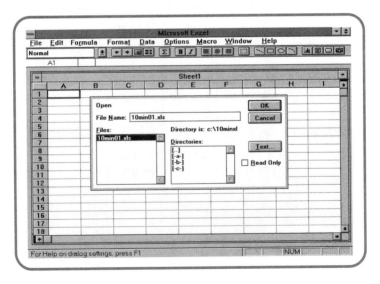

Figure 4-3. *Opening an existing worksheet.*

Saving an Existing Excel Worksheet

Saving an existing worksheet is similar to saving a new worksheet, except that you don't have to name the worksheet. Follow these steps:

1. Pull down the File menu.

2. Select the Save option.

Excel automatically saves your worksheet with its current name.

Saving a file with function keys The ALT+SHIFT+F2 function key combination will automatically save an existing file.

In this lesson you learned how to create, open, and save worksheets. In the next lesson you will learn how to enter and edit data in your worksheet.

Entering and Editing Data

In this lesson you'll learn how to enter data into your Excel worksheet and edit existing data.

Types of Data

There are four types of data you can use in Excel. They are:

Numbers   Numbers can be in a variety of forms; all numbers can be manipulated mathematically

Text   Text can contain both letters and numbers; text cannot be manipulated mathematically

Dates   Dates are specially formatted numbers

Formulas   Formulas tell Excel how to perform calculations using data in other cells

All data can be formatted in a variety of styles. Formatting and styles are discussed in later lessons.

Entering Data

Entering data is as simple as selecting a particular cell and typing input from the keyboard. For now, we will concentrate on numbers, texts, and dates. Formulas will be discussed in Lesson 6.

Use the following steps to enter data into a cell.

1. Move the cursor to a cell, using either the mouse or the keyboard arrow keys.

2. Begin typing. The data that you type will appear in the cell and the Formula bar, as shown in Figure 5-1.

3. When you finish typing, press Enter to accept the data.

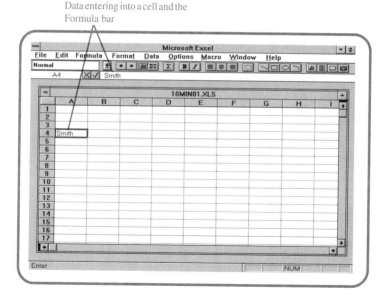

Figure 5-1. Entering data into an empty cell.

Canceling a data entry You can cancel your data entry at any time *before* pressing the Enter key simply by pressing Esc.

Excel will format your data depending on what was entered into the cell:

- If you typed any letters, the data will be formatted as *text*.

- If you typed only numbers, the data will be formatted as a *number*.

- If you typed numbers separated by the "-" or "/" characters (such as "12-31" or "1/2/92"), the data will be formatted as a *date*. Figure 5.2 shows an example of each of the data formats.

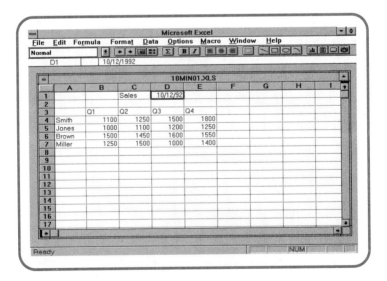

Figure 5-2. A sample worksheet with data entered.

Editing Data

Editing your data is a fairly simple exercise. Simply select the data you wish to change, then edit that data in the *Formula bar.* Follow these steps:

1. Move to the cell with the data that needs to be edited.

2. Move to the Formula bar.

3. Move the cursor to the data you wish to edit.

4. Use the Delete and Backspace keys to delete characters; type in replacement data if necessary.

5. Press Enter when you are finished editing. Your changes are accepted into the selected cell.

For this exercise, change the contents of cell B4 from **1000** to **1100.** (See Figure 5-3.)

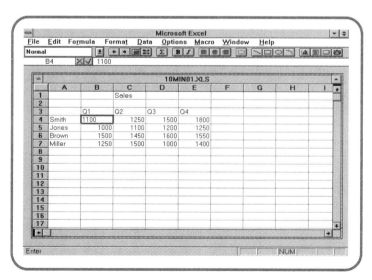

Figure 5-3. *Making changes in the cell and Formula bar.*

Saving your changes Be sure to save your work or you will lose all your changes.

In this lesson you learned how to enter and edit data in your worksheet. In the next lesson you will learn how to enter formulas and functions.

Lesson 6
Entering Formulas

In this lesson you'll learn how to manipulate data with mathematical formulas.

Now that you've entered numbers into your worksheet, you need to work with those numbers to create other numbers. Formulas allow you to calculate your data using addition, subtraction, multiplication, and division. You can also use advanced formulas preprogrammed into Excel; these advanced formulas are called functions and are explained in the next lesson.

> **Formula** A formula is a mathematical expression that defines the relationship between two or more values. In Excel formulas are used to calculate values for specific cells, and can use common mathematical operators, as well as references to other cells in the worksheet.

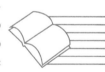

Entering Formulas

Formulas are used to calculate the values of data entered into other cells in your worksheet. A formula can consist of the contents of other cells (referred to by the cell reference), other numbers, and mathematical operators.

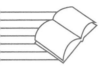 **Cell reference** The cell reference is simply the location of a particular cell. Each cell is referenced by the intersection of a column and a row; thus the top left cell is called A1 (for column A, row 1). The cell reference for the current cell is always listed in the Reference area of the worksheet window.

Excel formulas are comprised of three elements:

- An equals sign (=); this = sign is necessary at the start of each formula.

- One or more cell references, or a specific number.

- A mathematical operator (such as + or –); this is needed if your formula contains more than one cell reference or number.

Note that Excel formulas can contain common algebraic expressions, and follow common algebraic conventions and logic. Table 6-1 lists the accepted operators for Excel formulas.

Table 6-1. Accepted Operators for Excel Formulas.

Operator	Description
+	Addition
–	Subtraction
*	Multiplication
/	Division
^	Exponentiation

Table 6-2 shows some representative Excel formulas.

Table 6-2. Representative Excel Formulas.

Formula	Result
=2	Places the value 2 in the selected cell
=A1	Places the value of cell A1 in the selected cell
=A1*2	Places the value of cell A1 multiplied by 2 in the selected cell
=A1/2	Places the value of cell A1 divided by 2 in the selected cell
=A1+A2	Places the value of cell A1 plus the value of cell A2 in the selected cell
=(A1+A2)/2	Places the value of cell A1 plus the value of cell A2, all divided by 2, in the selected cell

To enter a formula in a cell, follow these steps:

1. Move the cursor to a cell.

2. Type = to start the formula.

3. Type the rest of the formula; remember to include cell references such as B4+B5+B6+B7. Note that the formula appears in the Formula bar as you type (see Figure 6-1).

4. Press Enter to accept the formula or Esc to reject the formula. When the formula is accepted, the result appears in the selected cell.

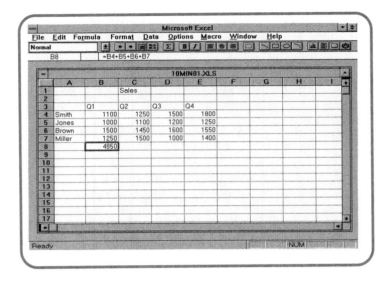

Figure 6-1. *Creating a formula.*

Using the mouse to create formulas Instead of typing in each cell reference, you can simply use the mouse to point to the cell you wish to refer to in your formula. If you use the mouse, you can also use the Enter button at the top of the window to accept the formula, instead of pressing the Enter key.

In this lesson you learned how to enter simple formulas into an Excel worksheet. In the next lesson you will learn how to use Excel's built-in functions to simplify the creation of complex formulas.

Lesson 7

Using Functions and the Auto-sum Tool

In this lesson you'll learn how to use Excel's built-in functions, as well as the new Auto-sum feature.

Using Excel's Built-in Functions

Functions simplify the creation of complex formulas. In the example shown in Lesson 6, you had to type =B4+B5+B6+B7 to sum a column of numbers. Excel includes a built-in function called *SUM* that lets you sum a column or row of numbers without having to type every cell into the formula.

Function A function is a type of formula built-in to the Excel system. You can use Excel's built-in functions instead of writing complex formulas in your worksheets. You can also include functions as part of your formulas.

An Excel function uses the following format:

The equal sign (=), the function, and the function argument (within parentheses)

For example, to sum the column of numbers referd to above using a function, you would type:

=SUM(B4:B7)

The function argument now consists of a *range reference.* In essence, this formula tells Excel to sum the range from cell B4 to cell B7.

Using Range References

You can save time and effort by unsing a range references in you formulas. A range reference is expressed by listing the first and last cells in the range, separated by a colon (:). The reference B4:B7, for example, refers to the range of cells between and including B4 and B7. When entering a formula, the range reference may either be entered manually or by selecting the range with the mouse or keyboard.

To select a range with the mouse:

1. Place the mouse pointer in the first cell of the range.

2. Press and hold the left mouse button.

3. Drag the mouse pointer to the last cell of the range and release the mouse button. The range is now highlighted, as shown in Figure 7-1.

Range references A range reference is a collection of adjacent cells. These may be in a column, a row, or a larger area consisting of several rows and columns.

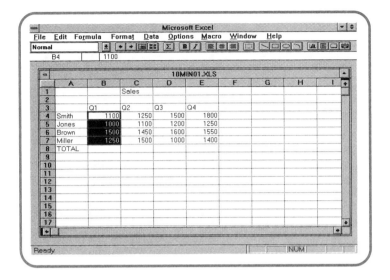

Figure 7-1. *A range of cells highlighted.*

Using the Formula Paste Function

You can enter a function into a formula either by typing the name of the function or by pasting the function into the formula using a list of functions. Pasting a function from Excel's built-in list is helpful when you can't remember the function's proper name. To access this list of functions, use the Formula Paste Function command.

To use the Formula Paste Function command, follow these steps:

1. Move the cursor into a cell.

2. Pull down the Formula menu.

3. Select the Paste Function option.

4. Select a function from the list in the Paste Function dialog box (see Figure 7-2). Every Excel function is listed, followed by parentheses for the range reference.

5. Excel automatically places the cursor between the parentheses in the Formula bar. Enter the applicable range reference between the parentheses.

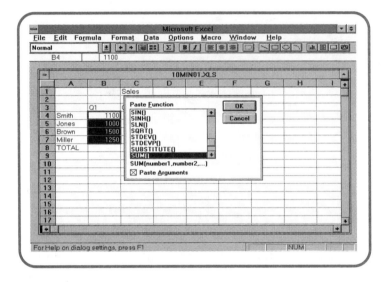

Figure 7-2. *Using the Formula Paste Function option.*

A list of common Excel functions are included in the back of this book.

Using the Auto-sum Feature

One of the most used functions is the SUM function. If you are like most Excel users, you will find that over half of your formulas involve totaling rows or columns of numbers. That's why an Auto-sum button was added to the new Excel 3 Tool bar.

The Auto-sum button inserts a formula (using the SUM function) in the cell at the end of a row or column of numbers. Auto-sum attempts to determine which data is to be totaled, usually by selecting the associated range of numbers near the current cell. If Auto-sum selects an incorrect range of cells to total, you can still insert the correct range reference between the parentheses in the formula.

Correcting Auto-sum Auto-sum merely suggests a range of cells to total. This range is not accepted until you press enter. At any time before accepting the formula you can manually select a range of cells, which is entered automatically between the parentheses in the formula created by Auto-sum.

To use Auto-sum, follow these steps:

1. Select a cell, preferably a cell at the end of a row or column of data.

2. Click the Auto-sum button in the Tool bar.

3. If the range selected by Auto-sum is correct, press Enter to accept the formula.

4. If the range selected is not correct, use the mouse or cursor keys to highlight a new range, then accept the formula.

5. Excel displays the result of the formula in the selected cell. (See Figure 7-3.)

Suggested range

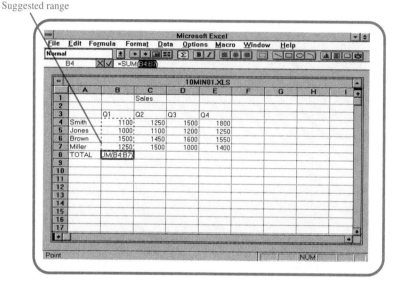

Figure 7-3. *Using Auto-sum to total a column of numbers.*

Using Auto-sum from the keyboard You can activate the Auto-sum feature from the keyboard by pressing ALT+=.

In this lesson you learned how to use functions and Auto-sum to easily create advanced formulas in your worksheet. In the next lesson you will learn how to work with named cells and ranges.

Lesson 8
Naming Cells and Ranges

In this lesson you'll learn how to assign names to cells and ranges and use named cells and ranges in formulas.

As you develop more complex formulas and use more advanced features such as sorting, inserting, and deleting, you may find it more convenient to attach a fixed *name* to a cell or range instead of using a variable cell or range reference. By naming cells you can refer to that name in a formula. That name is attached to the cell's *contents*, not its position so that your formulas won't change if you sort your data or add or delete rows or columns. It is also quicker to use a range name in a formula instead of a long range reference.

Naming a Cell

To assign a name to a specific cell, follow these steps:

1. Select the cell you wish to name.

2. Pull down the Formula menu.

3. Select the Define Name command.

4. When the dialog box in Figure 8-1 appears, accept the name Excel provides for you or enter a new one.

5. Select OK to accept the selection and close the dialog box.

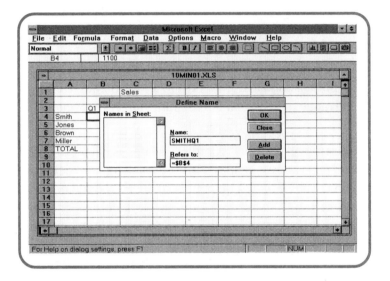

Figure 8-1. *Naming a cell.*

Naming a Range

Naming a range is similar to naming a cell. Follow these steps:

1. Select a range of cells.

2. Pull down the Formula menu.

3. Select the Define Name command.

4. When the dialog box appears, accept the name Excel provides for you or enter a new one.

5. Selct **OK** to accept the selection and close the dialog box.

Using the keyboard to assign names You can use CTRL+F3 to open the Formula Assign Name dialog box.

Using Named Cells in a Formula

You can use a named cell or range in place of a cell or range reference in a formula. Simply type in the name of the formula. For example, if you assigned the name SMITHQ1 to cell B4, the formula

=B4*2

becomes

=SMITHQ1*2

While this might seem like a lot of work, if you had referenced cell B4 in the formula then sorted the data, the *relative reference* would still refer to cell B4, even though the sort might have moved the cell contents to another location. By using a named cell (a kind of *absolute reference*), your formula will always point to the same data, no matter where that data is in the worksheet.

Correcting wrong names If you enter a name in a formula and Excel displays the message #NAME? in the selected cell, you have entered an incorrect name. You can either retype the name in the formula, or open the Formula Assign Names dialog box and choose the correct name from the named cells listed.

In this lesson you learned how to work with named cells and ranges. In the next lesson you will learn how to create a database.

Lesson 9
Creating a Database

In this lesson you'll learn how to create a database.

You can create a database from any Excel spreadsheet. Excel's database commands and functions let you organize, manipulate, and analyze in ways not possible with a normal Excel spreadsheet.

> **Database** A database is a tool for organizing and managing information. Databases are comprised of distinct data *records*, each with one or more data *fields*.

Planning a Database

An Excel database is really just an extension of an Excel worksheet. In fact, if your worksheets are planned properly, it is easy to convert a normal worksheet into a database. Figure 9-1 illustrates the parts of a database.

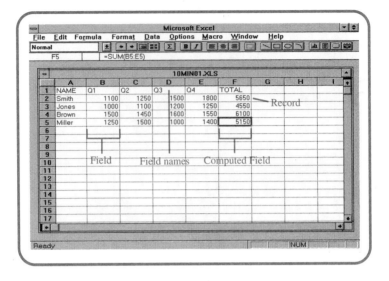

Figure 9-1. *The parts of a database.*

The following list details the parts of a database.

Database range   The range of worksheet cells defined as the database

Record   A single row in a database

Field   Each column of the database is *a field of the database;* each cell within a column *is a field of an individual record*

Computed field   A field containing formulas, functions, or references

Field name   Field names identify the data stored in a field

Proper database design A database *must* be arranged in the set order described above or it will not function properly. The first row of the database *must* contain field names.

Defining a Database

To turn your worksheet into a database, define a range of cells as the database range using the steps below:

1. Select the range of cells for your database. The top row of cells in the range must contain the field names; the last row of cells should be blank, for future expansion.

2. Pull down the Data menu.

3. Select the Set Database option.

Excel now knows to read this range whenever any database function or operation is performed.

Using multiple databases on a single worksheet Even though you can set up multiple databases on a single worksheet, you can use only one database at a time. You must redefine the database range each time you switch between databases.

Using Data Forms

You can add or manipulate information in a database just as you would in a normal worksheet. Excel also lets you use *data forms* to view, add, and edit records in your database.

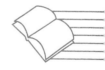

Data form A data form is a special Excel dialog box that displays the fields of a database. Each record is displayed in a separate dialog box, and you can easily switch from record to record.

Figure 9-2 displays the parts of a sample data form.

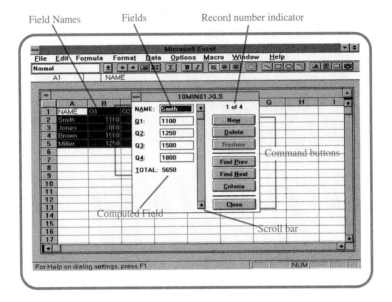

Figure 9-2. *A sample data form.*

The following list details the parts of a data form.

Field names   The field names from your database

Fields   The specific field data from individual records; you can edit this data directly in the field boxes (field data that is *not* displayed in text boxes are computed fields and cannot be edited)

Scroll bar   Lets you scroll from record to record through your database

Record number indicator	Indicates what record is displayed out of the total number of records in the database
Command buttons	Let you create new records, delete or restore the current record, find records that match a certain criteria, and close the data form

To display the data form for your current database, follow these steps:

1. Make sure your database range is defined.

2. Pull down the Data menu.

3. Select the Form option. Excel now displays the data form for the current database. You can view, edit, or delete the contents of the database, or use the New option to add records to the database.

4. When you finish, select the Close button to exit the data form.

Database range is not defined If you try to view a data form *before* you select a database range, Excel will display the message Database range is not defined. You need to back up and define your database range, as discussed earlier in this lesson, before you attempt to use any database operations.

In this lesson you learned how to create a database and use data forms. In the next lesson you will learn how to find specific data in the database as well as how to sort database records.

Lesson 10
Finding and Sorting Data

In this lesson you'll learn how to find data in a database and organize your data with the sort keys.

Finding Data with a Data Form

You can use a data form to find specific data in a database. To search for data, you must enter *criteria* that Excel can use to search for data in selected fields.

Criteria Criteria are instructions that specify types of data. Excel will search for data in a database that match specified criteria.

You can search for records using the following criteria:

Quantities You can use operators to search for numerical values; the operators available include:

=, equal to
>, greater than
<, less than
>=, greater than or equal to
<=, less than or equal to
<>, not equal

	for example, $<=1000$ will find all numerical values less than or equal to 1000
Characters	You can search for specific text, numbers, or logical values; for example, you can search for all occurences of the name Smith
Wild card characters	You can use a question mark (?) to find any single character; for example, Sm?th will find Smith, Smoth, Smyth. etc.; you can use an asterisk (*) to find any combination of characters; for example, Sm* will find Smith, Smooch, etc.

To search for data in a database, follow these steps:

1. Make sure your database range is defined.

2. Pull down the Data menu.

3. Select the Form option.

4. When the data form appears, select the Criteria button.

5. Type your search criteria into the appropriate field box or boxes using the arrow keys or the mouse to move from box to box (see Figure 10-1). Note that you can specify criteria for multiple fields.

6. To search forward through the database, select the Find Next button. Excel searches for the next record that matches your criteria.

7. To search backward through the database, select the Find Previous button. Excel searches for the first prior record that matches your criteria.

8. When you finish, select the Close button to exit the data form.

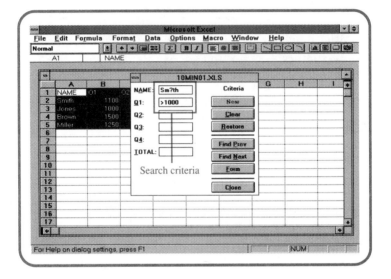

Figure 10-1. *Entering search criteria into a data form.*

No matching records If there are no matching records for your requested criteria, Excel beeps and displays the current record.

Using the Sort Command to Rearrange Your Data

Often you want your data to appear in a sorted order. Excel lets you sort your data either alphabetically or numerically, in either ascending or descending order. It also lets you perform multiple compound sorts, so that data is arranged in a nestled pattern.

> **Multiple compound sorts** A multiple compound sort involves sorting on more than one sort key. For example, you might want to sort by state first, then by city, and so on.

> **Fields to sort** You can use the sort feature on both database ranges and on normal worksheets. You must specify the sort range separately from the database range. *Do not select the field name row* as part of the sort range; if you do this the field names will become intermixed with the other rows of data in the selected range!

Sorting your data is as simple as selecting the range of data and using the Data Sort command. To sort a range of data, follow these steps:

1. Select the range of data to be sorted. Be sure to include all cells in a table *except* the column headings (field names).

2. Pull down the Data menu.

3. Select the Sort command.

4. When the dialog box in Figure 10-2 appears, use Tab to move to the column you wish to sort by. (Note that you can also sort by rows.)

5. Select whether your data will be sorted in ascending or descending order.

6. Click on **OK** or press Enter to sort the data.

Excel will now sort your data in the order you specified.

Figure 10-2. Sorting a range of data.

Undoing a sort If you forgot to highlight all of the data range—including the *row labels*—you could end up with a totally garbled mess of numbers. To undo a bad sort, pull down the Edit menu and select the Undo option. Your data will be returned to its former state.

Note that you can sort up to three different keys; in our example, you might want to sort by column A (last name), then column B (first quarter sales). You would simply fill in information for both the first and second sort keys in the dialog box.

In this lesson you learned how to find data in a database, as well as how to sort data. In the next lesson you will learn how to insert and delete cells in your worksheet.

Lesson 11
Inserting and Deleting Cells, Rows, and Columns

In this lesson you'll learn how to add and delete individual cells, rows, and columns to and from your worksheet.

Inserting Data

Sometimes you discover information that needs to be inserted into an existing worksheet. With the Insert command, you can insert individual cells or complete columns and rows.

Inserting Individual Cells

To insert an individual cell, follow these steps:

1. Position the cursor in the cell where you want to insert the new cell.

2. Pull down the Edit menu.

3. Select the Insert option.

4. When the dialog box in Figure 11-1 appears, indicate whether you want to shift the existing cells down or to the right.

5. Click on OK or press Enter to accept the command and Excel will automatically insert a blank cell in the worksheet and shift the existing cells as instructed.

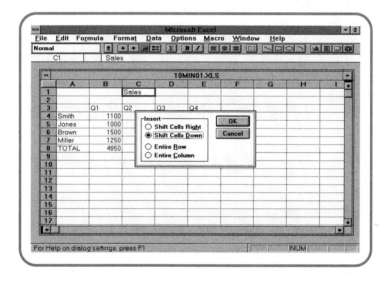

Figure 11-1. *Inserting a new cell.*

Inserting Rows and Columns

To insert a new row or column, follow these steps:

1. Position the cursor in the row or column heading where you want to insert a new row/column.

2. Click on the heading to select the entire row or column; the selection will be highlighted on-screen (see Figure 11-2).

3. Pull down the Edit menu.

4. Choose the Insert option; Excel automatically inserts the new row or column and shifts the existing row or column either down or to the right.

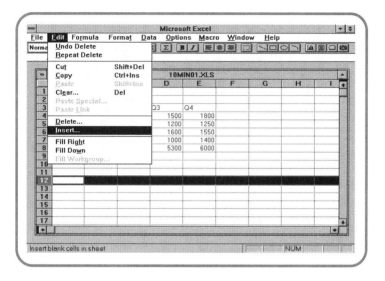

Figure 11-2. *Inserting a new row.*

Deleting Data

Deleting cells, rows, or columns is similar to inserting data; the only difference is choosing the Delete option from the Edit menu instead of the Insert option.

To delete data, follow these steps:

1. Highlight the cell, row, or column you wish to delete.

2. Pull down the Edit menu.

3. Select the Delete option.

4. If you are deleting an individual cell, instruct Excel to move the remaining cells either up or to the left.

 **Recovering deleted data** If you accidently delete data you want to keep, don't panic! Excel includes an Undelete option that lets you *undo* your last command. Simply pull down the Edit menu and select the Undo Delete option. You've now undone your last delete and your data is back where it belongs.

In this lesson you learned how to insert and delete cells in the worksheet. In the next lesson you will learn how to move and copy cells and ranges.

Lesson 12
Moving and Copying Cells and Ranges

In this lesson you'll learn how to use the Cut, Copy, and Paste commands to move and copy data on your worksheet.

There are times when you need to rearrange data on your worksheet. One way to rearrange data is to sort the data in a certain order, as discussed in Lesson 10. Another way is to use the Cut, Copy, and Paste commands.

Moving Data

Excel lets you move data from one place to another in your worksheet by cutting and pasting. The cut and paste procedure is similar to that used in other Windows applications.

To cut and paste data in your worksheet, follow these steps:

1. Select the cell or range to move. (You can cut individual cells, entire rows and columns, or marked cell ranges. Use your mouse or the keyboard to select the range.)

2. With the range highlighted, pull down the Edit menu.

3. Select the Cut option (see Figure 12-1).

4. Move the cursor to the first cell where you want to move your data. There is no need to select the entire range, just the first (upper left) cell of the range.

5. Pull down the Edit menu.

6. Select the Paste option. Excel moves the highlighted data to the new location (see Figure 12-2).

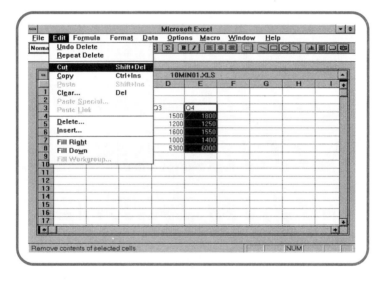

Figure 12-1. *Selecting a range of cells to cut.*

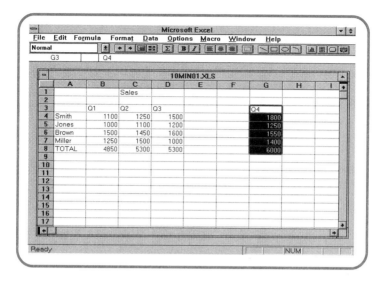

Figure 12-2. *The range of cells pasted to a new position.*

Copying over existing data Be careful! When you use the Paste command, Excel will paste the copied data over any data that previously existed in the target range. Make sure that no important data is in the target range.

Using the keyboard to cut and paste You can use the following keyboard shortcuts to cut and paste data: Cut is Shift+Delete and Paste is Enter.

Copying Data

Copying data is similar to moving data, except that both the original data and the copied data remain in your worksheet. You can use the Copy command to duplicate table headings or entire ranges of data.

To copy and paste data, follow these steps:

1. Select the cell or range to copy, using either the mouse or the keyboard.

2. With the range highlighted, pull down the Edit menu.

3. Select the Copy option.

4. Move the cursor to the first cell where you want to copy the data.

5. Pull down the Edit menu.

6. Select the Paste option. Excel copies the highlighted data to the new location.

Using the keyboard to copy and paste You can use the following keyboard shortcuts when copying and pasting data: Copy is Control+Delete and Paste is Enter.

In this lesson you learned how to copy and move data. In the next lesson you will learn how to change the size of rows and columns to accommodate data of varying lengths.

Lesson 13
Changing Column Width and Row Height

In this lesson you'll learn how to adjust column and row spacing.

Often you will find that you need to adjust your column or row size to fit large amounts of data or type sizes. With Excel you can adjust your column and row size with either the mouse or the keyboard, or you can let Excel adjust the size to automatically fit your data.

Changing Column Width with the Mouse

Using a mouse to change column width is similar to changing the size of a window in any Windows application. Follow these steps:

1. Move the mouse pointer to the heading at the top of the column you wish to adjust. Note that the mouse pointer changes shape as you move into this area of the worksheet window.

2. Move the mouse pointer to the line on the right border of the column (see Figure 13-1).

3. Hold down the left mouse button and drag the line to the right (to widen the column) or to the left (to shrink the column).

4. Release the mouse button to accept the new column width.

Positioning the column

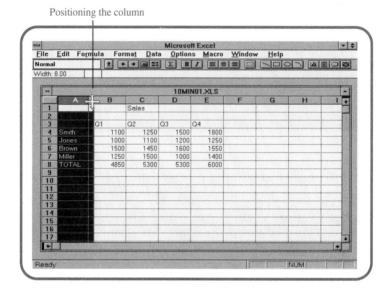

Figure 13-1. *Changing the column width with the mouse.*

Changing Column Width With the Keyboard

Although it is easier to adjust columns with the mouse, you can also adjust the size of columns using the menu system. Follow these steps:

1. Move the cursor to a cell in the column you wish to change.

2. Pull down the Format menu.

3. Select the Column Width option.

4. When the dialog box appears (see Figure 13-2), type the column width (in number of characters) into the space highlighted.

5. Press Enter to accept the new column width.

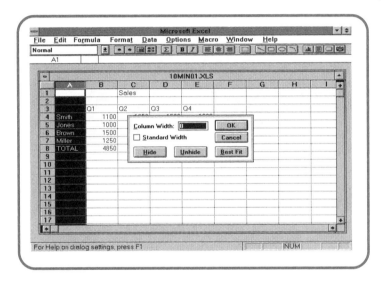

Figure 13-2. *Changing the column width with menu options.*

Automatically Adjusting Column Width

A new feature in Excel is the ability to have Excel automatically size columns to fit the largest chunk of data in any cell within the column. To automatically size a column, follow these steps:

1. Move the mouse pointer to the heading at the top of the column you want to adjust.

2. Now move the mouse pointer to the line at the right border of the column.

3. Double-click the left mouse button. Excel automatically adjusts the column width to fit your data.

Using the keyboard to accomplish the best fit You can also have Excel automatically adjust column size by selecting the Best Fit option in the Format Column Width dialog box.

Changing Row Height

When you change font size (discussed in later lessons), Excel will automatically adjust the row height to fit different type sizes. However, if you wish to change row height for effect, the operation is identical to that used when changing the column width.

To change row height with the mouse, follow these steps:

1. Move the mouse pointer to the heading on the left of the row you want to adjust.

2. Now move the mouse pointer to the line on the bottom border of the column.

3. Hold down the left mouse button and drag the line down or up until the row is at the desired height.

4. Release the mouse button to accept the new row height.

To change row height with the keyboard, follow these steps:

1. Move the cursor to any cell in the row you want to change.

2. Pull down the Format menu.

3. Select the Row Height option.

4. When the dialog box appears, type a row height into the space highlighted.

5. Press Enter to accept the new row height.

In this lesson you learned how to size rows and columns to fit your particular data. In the next lesson you will learn how to enhance your data using various text attributes.

Lesson 14

Enhancing Text with Bold, Italic, and Other Attributes

In this lesson you'll learn how to enhance your text with bold, italic, underline, and other attributes, using both the menu system and Tool Bar options.

In this lesson we begin examining the many ways to enhance the appearance of your worksheets, starting with text attributes.

Text attributes Text can be enhanced by appliying various *text attributes.* Two of the most common attributes are **bold** and *italic.* Attributes are often applied to add emphasis to specific text.

There are three ways to change text attributes: with the Tool bar, the Format Font command, or the keyboard shortcuts. Note that you change text attributes for an entire cell or range of cells; however, it is not possible to change attributes for selected characters *within* a cell.

Enhancing Text with the Tool Bar

Two of the most common text enhancements, bold and italic, are accessed from buttons on the Tool bar. To change text to bold or italic using the Tool bar, follow these steps:

1. Highlight the cell or range of cells.

2. Click on the bold or italic button on the Tool bar (see Figure 14-1).

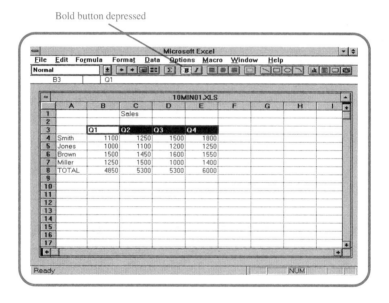

Figure 14-1. *Changing text to bold with the Tool bar.*

Changing text back to normal You can change enhanced text back to normal by clicking again on the Tool bar button; the button works like an on/off switch for text attributes.

67

Enhancing Text with the Format Font Command

There are additional text attributes that can be changed from the menu system. All text attributes (as well as font and color attributes) are accessed via the Format Font option. The Format Font dialog box lets you select the following attributes:

- **Bold**

- *Italic*

- Underline

- ~~Strikeout~~

To change text attributes using the menu system, follow these steps:

1. Highlight the cell or range.

2. Pull down the Format menu.

3. Select the Font option.

4. When the dialog box in Figure 14-2 appears, click on or off the attributes in the Style box.

5. Click on OK or press Enter to close the dialog box.

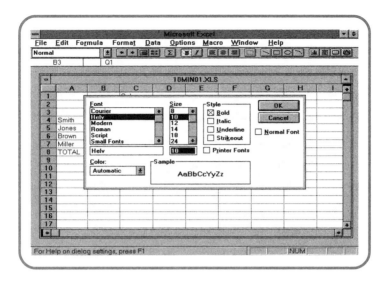

Figure 14-2. *Changing text attributes from the Format Font dialog box.*

Enhancing Text With the Keyboard

The following keyboard shortcuts can be used to change text attributes in selected cells or ranges.

Key Combination	Result
Ctrl+1	Returns text to normal
Ctrl+2	Bold
Ctrl+3	Italic
Ctrl+4	Underline
Ctrl+5	Strikeout

In this lesson you learned how to change text attributes. In the next lesson you will learn how to change fonts in your worksheet.

69

Lesson 15

Changing Fonts and Type Sizes

In this lesson you'll learn how to enhance the appearance of your worksheet by using font types.

Changing Fonts with the Format Font Command

To enhance the appearance of your worksheet, you can use different fonts and type sizes for parts of your document. To change the fonts and type sizes, simply use the Format Font command. Note that you can only change fonts for an entire cell or range of cells, not for selected text within a cell.

 Font The word *font* refers to the collection of properties inherent in a specific family of characters. Fonts contain the following characteristics: typeface, weight (Roman or bold), posture (upright or italic), and size.

Follow these steps to change fonts with the Format Font command:

1. Highlight the cell or range.

2. Pull down the Format menu.

3. Select the Font option and the dialog box in Figure 15-1 appears. To choose from fonts that your printer can reproduce, click on the Printer Fonts box.

4. Select the font, type size and color (if available with your printer) you want.

5. Click on OK or press Enter to close the dialog box.

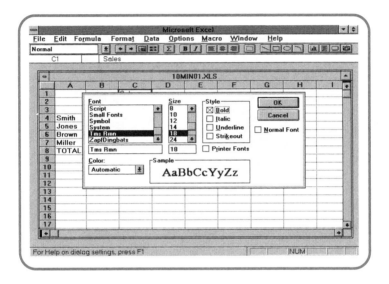

Figure 15-1. *Changing fonts with the Format Font dialog box.*

Making your printout resemble your screen display To ensure accurate reproduction of your on-screen worksheet, make sure that the Printer Fonts option is enabled.

In this lesson you learned how to change fonts and type sizes. In the next lesson you will learn how to align data within a cell.

Aligning Information in a Cell

In this lesson you'll learn how to use the Tool bar and menu options to change the alignment of your data.

Aligning Data

Another way to enhance the look of your worksheet is to make sure that your data is aligned properly. There are four alignments possible within Excel:

- Right align

- Left align

- Center

- General alignment

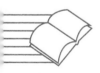

General alignment General alignment format makes all text left-aligned, all numbers right-aligned, and all logical and error values centered.

Figure 16-1 shows the three different types of alignment.

Left-aligned column   Centered columns   Right-aligned column

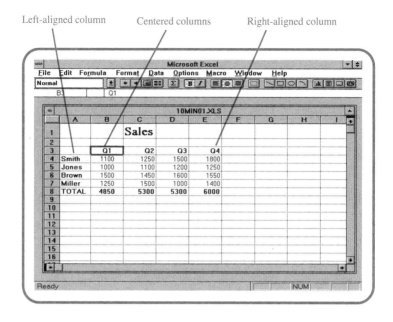

Figure 16-1. *Sample worksheet with columns left-aligned, right-aligned, and centered.*

You can use either the Tool bar or the Format Alignment command to align your data. To use the Tool bar to align data, follow these steps:

1. Highlight the cell or range.

2. Click on the proper alignment button in the Tool bar. Excel automatically aligns all data in the selected cells.

To use the menu system to align data, follow these steps:

1. Highlight the cell or range.

2. Pull down the Format menu.

73

3. Select the Alignment option.

4. Select the proper alignment box.

This dialog box also includes options that let you Fill selected cells by repeating their contents (useful for creating rows of dashes or lines) and Wrap long lines of text within single cells.

In this lesson you learned how to align your data. In the next lesson you will learn how to change number formats.

Lesson 17
Changing Number Formats

In this lesson you'll learn how to format your data with different number formats.

Number Formats

There are numerous ways to express a number. A number can be expressed as a whole number, a percent, a fraction, currency, a date, or an exponent. Excel has a wide variety of number formats that you can apply to your data.

Table 17-1 lists some of the number formats along with examples of their effect.

Table 17-1. Sample number formats.

Format	Number typed			
	5000	5	–5	.5
General	5000	5	–5	0.5
0	5000	5	–5	1
0.00	5000.00	5.00	–5.00	0.50
#,##0	5,000	5	–5	1
#,##0.00	5,000.00	5.00	–5.00	0.50
$#,##0_.00; ($#,##0.00)	$5,000.00	$5.00	($5.00)	$0.50

(continued)

Table 17-1. (continued)

Format	Number typed			
	5000	**5**	**–5**	**.5**
0%	500000%	500%	–500%	50%
0.00%	500000.00%	500.00%	–500.00%	50.00%
0.00E+00	5.00E+03	5.00E+00	–5.00E+00	5.00E–01
# ?/?	5000	5	–5	1/2

Table 17-2 lists some of the data formats, with examples.

Table 17-2. Sample data formats.

Format	Display
m/d/yy	2/14/92
d-mmm-yy	14-Feb-92
d-mmm	14-Feb
mmm-yy	Feb-92
h:mm AM/PM	9:42 PM
h:mm:ss AM/PM	9:42:27 PM
h:mm	21:42
h:mm:ss	21:42:27
m/d/yy h:mm	2/14/92 21:42

Applying Number Formats

Excel applies the General number format globally when you enter numbers into your worksheet. You can apply any number format to any cell you select.

To apply a number format, follow these steps:

1. Highlight the cell or range.

2. Pull down the Format menu.

3. Select the Number option.

4. When the dialog box in Figure 17-1 appears, select a format from the list presented. (You can use the scroll bars to scroll through the available formats.)

5. Click on OK or press Enter to close the dialog box.

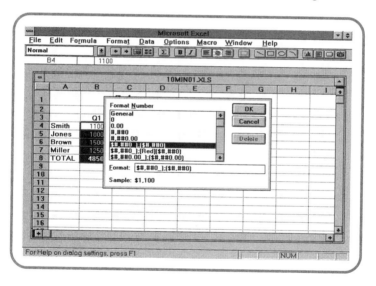

Figure 17-1. *Applying number formats.*

Creating New Number Formats

In spite of the wide variety of number formats available, there will be times when none of the built-in formats are ideal for your needs. Fortunately you can also instruct Excel to create custom number formats. For example, you might want to create a percent format that displays just one digit past the decimal point, like this: 0.0%.

To create a new number format, follow these steps:

1. Highlight the cell or range.

2. Pull down the Format menu.

3. Select the Number option.

4. When the dialog box appears, scroll to the end of the list of built-in formats. (The mouse pointer will change to the text writing tool.)

5. Type your new format in the space provided.

6. Click on OK or press Enter to close the dialog box. Your data is now formatted with the new number format.

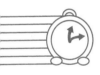

Editing existing formats You can also create new number formats by editing existing formats in the dialog box. When you close the dialog box your new format will be added to the bottom of the list, and the original format will also appear, unchanged.

In this lesson you learned how to apply and create number formats. In the next lesson you will learn how to enhance the appearance of your worksheet by adding borders and shading to selected cells.

Adding Borders and Shading to Cells and Ranges

In this lesson you'll learn how to enhance the appearance of your worksheet by adding borders and shading to cells and ranges.

So far you've learned how to format numbers and text in Excel. You can add even more pizazz to your worksheet by adding borders and shading to individual cells or ranges of cells. Borders and shading are useful when you want to highlight information in a worksheet or when you want to add lines between rows or columns of data. Use the Format Border command to add both borders and shading; you can also use the Format Pattern command to change the type of shading used.

Adding Borders to Cells

The Format Border command has five options for adding a border to a cell or range of cells. These are:

Outline   Adds a border around the entire selected area

Left   Adds a border on the left edge of every cell in the selected area

Right   Adds a border on the right edge of every cell in the selected area

Top   Adds a border on the top edge of every cell in the selected area

Bottom   Adds a border on the bottom edge of every cell in the selected area

The Format Border dialog box (see Figure 18-1) also lets you add shading to the selection and set the color and the style of the border. An example of each style is shown in the dialog box as well.

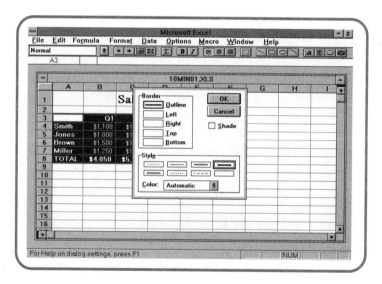

Figure 18-1. *The Format Border dialog box.*

Note that adding any border except an outline border to a range of cells adds that border to every cell in the range.

For example, adding a left border to a range of cells three columns wide adds left borders to all the cells in all three columns. The exception is the outline border. Adding an outline border to a range of cells adds a border around the entire range, not individual cells within the range. See Figure 18-2 for examples of various types of borders.

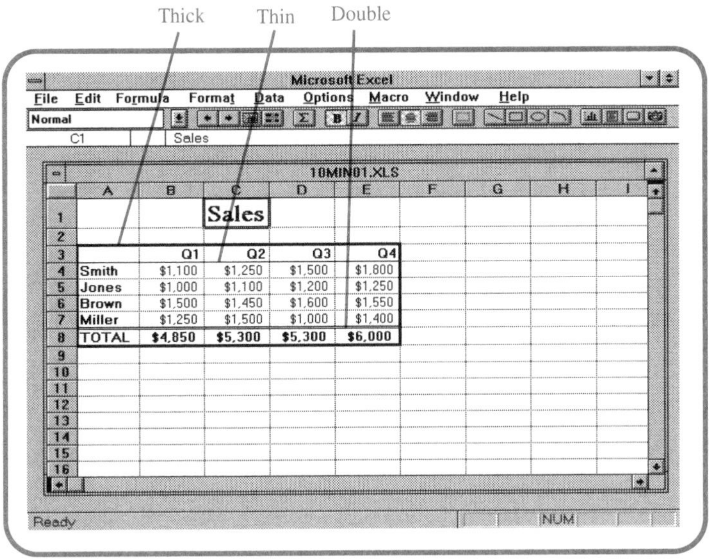

Figure 18-2. *Examples of various borders.*

To add a border to a cell or group of cells, follow these steps:

1. Highlight the cell or range.

2. Pull down the Format menu.

3. Select the Border option.

4. Select the type of border, border style, and border color.

81

5. Click on OK or press Enter to close the dialog box. Excel automatically adds the border to the selected cells.

 **Conflicting borders on adjoining cells** Remember that adjoining cells share borders. For example, adding a top border on one cell has the same effect as adding a bottom border on the cell above it. If two cells share a border but each cell has a different border style applied, only one border style will be visible. If this occurs, you might want to reformat one or both of the cells to avoid this type of border conflict.

Adding Shading to Cells

Adding shading to cells is also accomplished with the Format Borders command, in fact, Excel regards shading as just another type of border. To add shading to a cell or range of cells, follow these steps:

1. Highlight the cell or range.

2. Pull down the Format menu.

3. Select the Border option.

4. Turn on the Shade check box.

5. Click on OK or press Enter to close the dialog box. Excel automatically adds shading to the selected cells.

You can also change the type of shading applied to the selected cells. You can change background color, foreground color, and the shading pattern. Note that to use this option, you must be using full menus.

To change shading patterns, follow these steps:

1. Highlight the cell or range of cells.

2. Pull down the Format menu.

3. Select the Patterns option.

4. When the dialog box in Figure 18-3 appears, select the foreground/background color combination and the shading pattern desired. If you select the Automatic option, Excel uses the default black/white combination and pattern.

5. Click on OK or press Enter to close the dialog box. Excel automatically applies the new shading pattern to the selected cells.

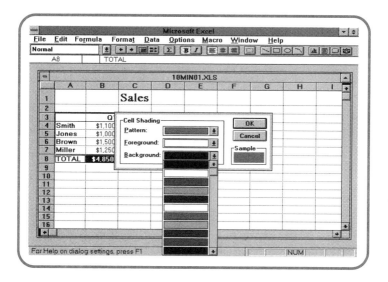

Figure 18-3. Changing shading patterns in the Format Patterns dialog box.

In this lesson you learned how to use borders and shading to enhance your worksheet. In the next lesson you will learn how to combine all the worksheet enhancements into one easy to use style command.

Lesson 19
Using Styles to Enhance Work- sheets

In this lesson you'll learn how to use cell styles to automate the formatting of your worksheet.

Styles

In the last few lessons you learned several ways to enhance the appearance of your worksheet. Excel 3 lets you combine all of these enhancements into a single cell *style*. Styles are an easy and powerful way to apply identical sophisticated enhancements in multiple areas of your worksheet.

Styles A style is a combination of all available cell formats.

Each style is made up of six different formatting attributes:

- Number

- Font

- Alignment

- Border

- Pattern

- Protection

You are now familiar with each of these enhancements except *protection;* the protection option lets you *lock* a cell to keep its contents from being changed or *hide* a cell to prevent the cell's formula from being displayed in the Formula bar. Generally this is an option for advanced users.

Each of these enhancements can be included or excluded in a given style. If you exclude an enhancement, Excel uses a general format for that attribute. If you include an enhancement, you can set all available options for that attribute.

 Style Precedence When you apply a style to a cell, all existing formats applied to that cell are overidden by the new style. If you apply a style first and then add extra formats, however, the new formats override those formats attached to the style.

The ability to apply styles to selected cells in your worksheet is a powerful tool. Mastering the use of styles will make you more efficient and adept at producing quality worksheets.

Applying Existing Styles

Excel lists four built-in styles in the Tool bar's style list.

Normal   This is the default style, applied to all cells in new worksheets; the Normal style has all options turned on, with the following formats:

Number—General
Font—Helvetica 10
Alignment—General
Borders—None
Pattern—No shading
Protection—Locked

Comma   All options turned off except:

Number—#,##0.00

Currency   All options turned off except:

Number—
$#,##0.00_);[RED]($#,##0.00)

Percent   All options turned off except:

Number—0%

You can apply a style in one of two ways: by using the style list in the Tool bar, or by using the Format Style command.

Using the Tool bar is the easiest way to apply styles. Follow these steps:

1. Highlight the cell or range of cells.

2. Click the arrow to the right of the style list in the Tool bar; the style list will drop down to display all available styles (see Figure 19-1).

3. Click on the style. Excel automatically applies that style to the selected cells.

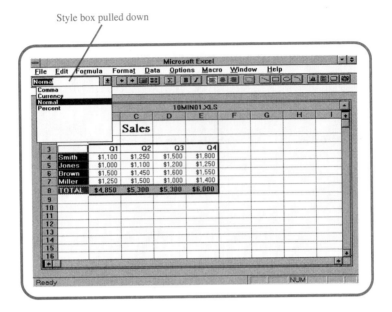

Style box pulled down

Figure 19-1. *Applying styles with the Tool bar.*

While using the Tool bar to apply styles is fast, using the Format Style command is more thorough. When you use the Format Style command to apply a style, the Format Style dialog box displays a description of the formats contained in the style.

To apply a style with the Format Style command, follow these steps:

1. Highlight the cell or range of cells.

2. Pull down the Format menu.

3. Select the Style option.

4. When the dialog box in Figure 19-2 appears, select the style from the Style Name box.

5. Click on OK or press Enter to close the dialog box. Excel automatically applies the style to the selected cells.

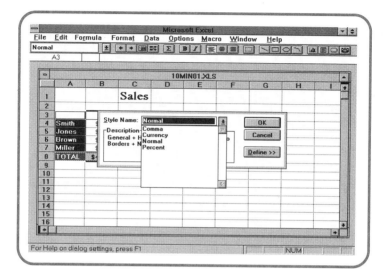

Figure 19-2. *Applying styles with the Format Style command.*

In this lesson you learned how to enhance your worksheet with styles. In the next lesson you will learn how to create and modify styles.

Creating Custom Styles

In this lesson you'll learn how to create and modify your own styles.

You are not limited to the built-in styles included with Excel. You can create any number of custom styles, each with its own unique combination of format enhancements.

You can create custom styles either by example or by definition. We will examine both methods.

Creating Styles by Example

This method is used if you have already used the Format menu commands to enhance a cell with a combination of formats. Excel lets you create a style based on that format combination by selecting the cell and assigning the combination of formats a style name.

The easiest way to create a style by example is with the Tool bar. Follow these steps:

1. Select a cell that contains the combination of formats.

2. Move the cursor to the current (displayed) style in the Tool bar's style list and highlight the style name.

3. Type a new name for this style.

4. Press Enter. Excel assigns the new style name to the selected combination of formats.

Using existing styles Instead of always creating totally new styles for your worksheets, Excel gives you the option of redefining existing styles. This method is identical to creating a new style, except you don't assign a new name to the altered style. The *new* style keeps the old name, and the formatting of all cells with that style applied are updated with the new formats automatically.

Creating Styles by Definition

This method of creating a style lets you specify a combination of formats by using the Format Style command. Follow these steps:

1. Pull down the Format menu.

2. Choose the Style option.

3. Select the Define button; the dialog box expands (see Figure 20-1).

4. Type a name for your new style in the Style Name box.

5. Turn off the check boxes for those attributes you don't want included in the style.

6. Turn on the check boxes for those attributes you do want included in the style.

7. To change the formats for any of the attributes, select the corresponding button for that attribute.

8. When the separate dialog boxes for the text attributes appear, select the formats for each attribute.

9. Press Enter to close the attribute dialog box.

10. Repeat steps 7 and 8 for any other attributes you wish to change.

11. Click on OK or press Enter to close the dialog box. Excel creates a new style based on your input.

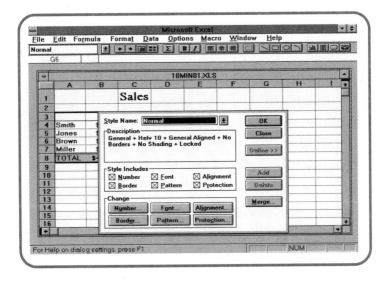

Figure 20-1. *The expanded Format Style dialog box.*

Changing the Normal style If you want to change the format of all the cells in your worksheet at one time, simply redefine the Normal style. Since the Normal style is the default style, all cells without additional styles applied will be updated to reflect any format changes you apply when you redefine the Normal style.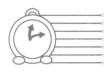

In this lesson you learned how to use styles to quickly apply sophisticated formats to your worksheets. In the next lesson you will learn about creating charts.

In this lesson you'll learn how to create different types of charts with Excel and combine them with your data on one worksheet.

Excel has always been known for its ability to quickly create presentation-quality charts from worksheet data. Excel 3.0 adds tools that speed up the charting operation, create a greater variety of charts, and allow you to combine charts with your worksheets on a single page of output.

Chart A chart is a visual depiction of numerical data. The chart types available include pie charts, area charts, line charts, bar charts, and scatter charts.

Creating a New Chart

When you create a chart, the chart can be either created as a stand-alone file or incorporated as part of your worksheet. Procedures for both operations involve highlighting the range of cells to be charted, and then opening a new chart file to graphically depict the selected data.

To create a stand-alone chart, follow these steps:

1. Select the data range.

2. Pull down the File menu.

3. Select the New option.

4. When the dialog box in Figure 21-1 appears, select the Chart option.

5. Select OK to close the dialog box; Excel creates a bar chart in a new window, based on the selected data.

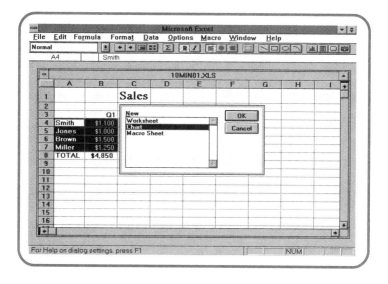

Figure 21-1. *Creating a stand-alone chart with the File New command.*

To incorporate a chart into your existing worksheet, follow these steps:

1. Select the data range.

2. Select the Chart button in the Tool bar.

3. Use the mouse to select the area of the worksheet where the chart will be placed; do this by moving the mouse pointer to the top left corner of the new area, pressing the left mouse button, dragging the mouse pointer to the bottom opposite corner of the area, and releasing the mouse button. (See Figure 21-2)

When you release the mouse button, Excel creates a chart and places it in the *frame* you created on your worksheet.

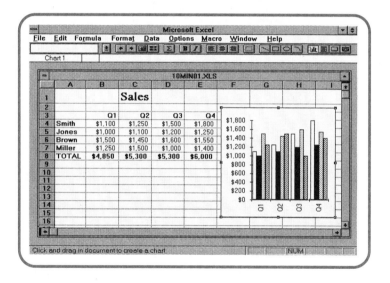

Figure 21-2. *Creating a new chart and placing it within an existing worksheet.*

Exploring the Chart Window

To make any changes to the newly created chart, you must first enter the chart window. If you incorporated the new chart into your worksheet, you must double-click on the chart frame to open the window containing the new chart.

The chart window is similar to the normal worksheet window except for some changes in the Menu bar. The chart window menu bar, shown in Figure 21-3, includes the following pull-down menus:

Chart window menu bar

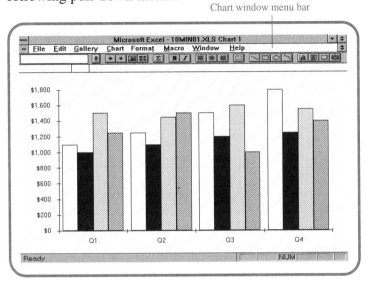

Figure 21-3. The chart window.

File   Identical to the worksheet File menu

Edit   Identical to the worksheet Edit menu

Gallery   Displays types of charts available within Excel

Chart   Allows you to add elements to your chart

Format   Allows you to edit and format chart elements

Macro   Identical to the worksheet Macro menu

Window   Identical to the worksheet Window menu

Help   Identical to the worksheet Help menu

Selecting a Chart Type

Excel automatically creates a bar chart when you create a new chart. The bar chart is set as the *preferred* chart type. While a bar chart is ideal for many situations, you fortunately have the option of selecting from other types of charts.

To change the type of your chart, follow these steps:

1. With the chart window open, pull down the Gallery menu (see Figure 21-4).

2. Select a new chart type from the choices presented.

3. Excel now displays a gallery of available chart formats for the type of chart you selected (see Figure 21-5). Select the chart format by double-clicking on that format.

Excel automatically changes your chart to the type and format selected.

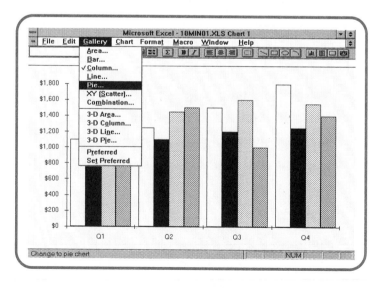

Figure 21-4. Selecting a new chart type.

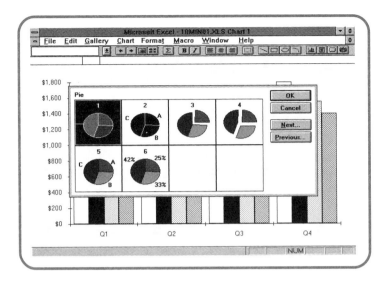

Figure 21-5. *The gallery of formats for the pie chart type.*

To return to the worksheet, either click anywhere on the worksheet (if the worksheet is visible), or select the worksheet file name from the Windows pull-down menu.

Saving a chart If you choose to save the chart as a separate file, follow the same procedures for saving a worksheet file. If you incorporate the chart as part of the existing worksheet, however, the chart will be automatically saved when you save the worksheet file.

In this lesson you learned how to create a chart and select a chart type. In the next lesson you will learn how to enhance your chart with formatting options.

Lesson 22
Formatting Charts

In this lesson you'll learn how to use the formatting options to enhance the appearance of your charts.

The chart that Excel automatically creates from your data is very plain. In the last lesson you learned how to select from a variety of chart types and formats. Excel has other options that let you further enhance that chart to more effectively present your data visually.

Adding a Legend

In some cases you need to add a *legend* to clarify the data represented in your chart. Excel lets you easily add legends and other types of text to your existing chart.

Legend A legend explains the meaning of a series of data points in your chart.

To add a legend to your chart, follow these steps:

1. With the chart window open, pull down the Chart menu.

2. Select the Add Legend option.

Excel adds the legend to your chart, as shown in Figure 22-1.

100

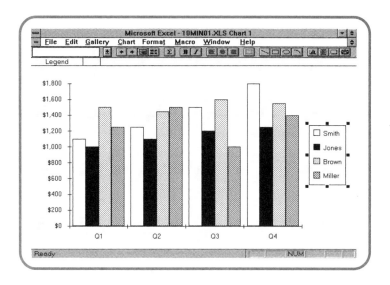

Figure 22-1. *An Excel chart with legend added.*

Deleting a legend To delete an existing legend, simply pull down the Chart menu and select the Delete Legend option.

You can move the legend to another position on your chart by selecting the legend with the mouse and dragging it to a new position. You can also move the legend using menu options by following these steps:

1. With the chart window open, select the legend.

2. Pull down the Format menu.

3. Select the Legend option.

4. Select the legend position.

5. Click on OK or press Enter to close the dialog box and reposition the legend.

101

Adding Chart Titles

To add a title to your chart, follow these steps:

1. With the chart window open, pull down the Chart menu.

2. Select the Attach Text option.

3. Select the Chart Title option and close the dialog box.

4. The word title now appears at the top center of your chart (see Figure 22-2). Move the cursor to the formula bar to edit the title text. Press Enter to accept the new text.

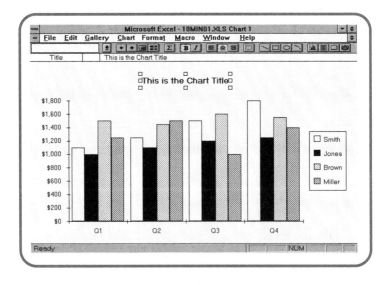

Figure 22-2. *A title added to the chart.*

Formatting Text and Other Chart Items

Now that you've added a legend and title to your chart, you may wish to change the chart's formats. The procedure is similar for editing almost all of the chart items: select the item and then select the appropriate action from the Format menu.

To edit the font of an object, follow these steps:

1. With the chart window open, select the object.

2. Pull down the Format menu.

3. Select the Font option.

4. Select the options and then close the dialog box.

To edit the border and area pattern of an object, follow these steps:

1. With the chart window open, select the object.

2. Pull down the Format menu.

3. Select the Patterns option.

4. Select the options and then close the dialog box.

As you experiment with various formatting options, you will discover that Excel allows you the flexibility to create an almost limitless variety of charts. If the default charts don't suit your style, create your own custom chart with the formatting options.

Formatting the Chart Frame in the Worksheet

Not only can you format the elements of your chart, you can also format the chart frame in your worksheet. Excel considers the frame an independent graphic object, and lets you apply various object formatting options to the frame.

Full menus You must be using full menus (which display all options and commands) to format a chart frame (or any other graphic object).

To format the chart frame, the worksheet window must be open. Follow these steps:

1. Select the chart frame.

2. Pull down the Format menu.

3. Select the Patterns option.

4. Select the border and fill options and click on OK or press Enter to close the dialog box.

Figure 22-3 shows a worksheet with a formatted chart frame.

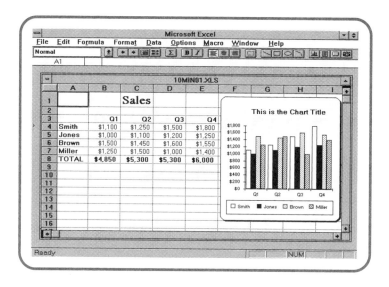

Figure 22-3. *A chart frame with a rounded, shadowed border.*

In this chapter you learned how to enhance the look of your charts. In the next chapter you will learn how to use the 3-D charting options.

Lesson 23
Working with 3-D Charts

In this lesson you'll learn how to use specific techniques for creating 3-D charts.

One of the new features of Excel 3.0 is the ability to create 3-D charts. The types of 3-D charts available range from simple bar and pie charts displayed with a three-dimensional perspective to complex charts with multicategory series. Figure 23-1 shows a simple pie chart with 3-dimensional perspective applied.

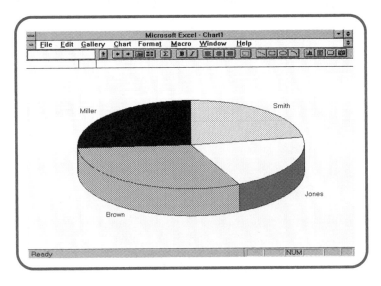

Figure 23-1. A simple pie chart with 3-D perspective.

Selecting 3-D Chart Types

Excel lets you choose four 3-D chart types from the Gallery pull-down menus:

- 3-D area

- 3-D column

- 3-D line

- 3-D pie

Of these types, the area, column, and pie types have formats that add the three-dimensional perspective to normal 2-D charts. The area, column, and line types have formats that incorporate multicategory data plotting.

To select a 3-D chart, follow these steps:

1. With the chart window open, pull down the Gallery menu.

2. Select one of the four 3-D options.

3. Select the chart format from the options presented.

Plotting a Multicategory 3-D Chart

When you have two or more sets of values to represent visually, you can either plot the data as a 2-D scatter chart or as a multicategory 3-D chart.

Multicategory chart A multicategory chart relates two or more sets of data simultaneously. Also referred to as an XY chart, these charts plot data in a three-dimensional plane among three axes.

Figure 23-2 is a 3-D column chart showing the relationship between related sets of data.

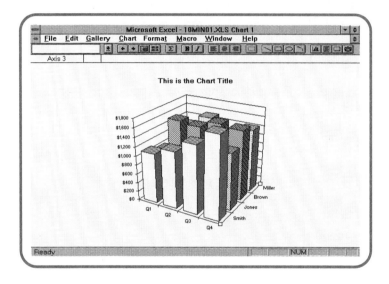

Figure 23-2. *Multicategory data plotted in a 3-D column chart.*

Changing the 3-D View

When creating a 3-D chart, you will find that you might want to vary the angle, elevation, or perspective of the chart to better show the individual data points. You can do this with the Format 3-D View command.

To change the 3-D view, follow these steps:

1. With the chart window open, pull down the Format menu.

2. Select the 3-D View option; the dialog box in Figure 23-3 appears.

3. To change the elevation of the chart, click on the up elevation or down elevation arrows. The wireframe chart in the dialog box will move to reflect your changes.

4. To change the rotation of the chart, click on the clockwise or counterclockwise rotation arrows. The wireframe chart in the dialog box will move to reflect your changes.

5. To change the 3-D perspective of the chart, click on the backward or forward perspective arrows. The wireframe chart in the dialog box will move to reflect your changes.

6. To see your changes in the chart *before* you accept the changes, click on the Apply button.

7. To accept your changes, click on the OK button or press Enter.

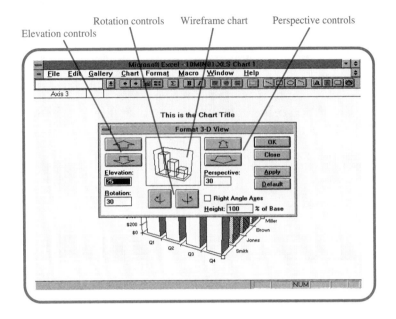

Rotation controls   Wireframe chart   Perspective controls
Elevation controls

Figure 23-3. *The Format 3-D View dialog box.*

Reverting to the original format You can
cancel the formatting operations at any time by
clicking on the Default button in the Format
3-D View dialog box.

Using values instead of direction arrows You
can type the precise values for elevation, rotation, and perspective directly into the text boxes
in the Format 3-D View dialog box. You can
also adjust the height as a percent of the base.

In this lesson you learned how to work with the 3-D
charts. In the next lesson you will learn how to enhance your
worksheet with text boxes and other graphic elements.

Lesson 24
Adding Text Boxes and Graphics to Worksheets

In this lesson you'll learn how to enhance the appearance of your worksheets with text boxes and graphic elements.

Excel 3.0 lets you annotate your worksheet with various graphic objects. The graphic objects available for your use are:

- Rectangles

- Ovals

- Arcs

- Lines and arrows

- Text boxes

Graphic object In Excel a graphic object is any nonworksheet object that is drawn on the worksheet. Graphic objects are used to enhance the appearance of a worksheet and draw attention to specific elements. A chart incorporated into a chart frame is handled like a graphic object.

111

Drawing Lines, Arcs, Ovals, and Rectangles

To draw all graphic objects:

1. Click on the drawing tool of your choice in the Tool bar. Note that the mouse pointer changes to a cross hair.

2. Position the cross hair in the upper left corner of the area where you want to draw the graphic object.

3. Press and hold the left mouse button and drag the mouse pointer until the object is the size and shape you want (see Figure 24-1).

4. Release the mouse button. The object is completed and automatically selected.

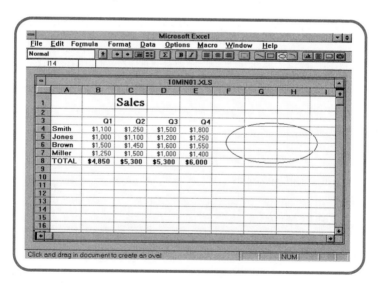

Figure 24-1. Drawing an oval.

Aligning objects while drawing You can re-strict lines to horizontal, vertical, or 45-degree angles by holding down the Shift key while drawing. This technique also produces perfect circles and squares while using the Circle, Arc and Rectangle tools.

Working with Text Boxes

Text boxes are drawn using the same technique as other graphic objects.

Text box A text box is a rectangular graphic object that incorporates text inside its borders. This text can be edited and formatted in the same manner as any other text.

To add text to a text box, follow these steps:

1. Position the cursor *inside* the text box.

2. Begin typing. Press Enter to start a new line, or the text will wrap automatically as you type (see Figure 24-2).

3. Leave the text box by moving the cursor anywhere *outside* the box.

113

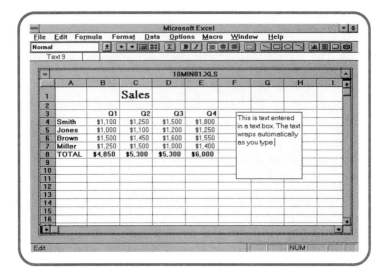

Figure 24-2. *Adding text to a text box.*

You can format text within a text box by highlighting the text with the cursor, then using any of the text formatting commands or buttons (on the Tool bar).

Moving, Sizing, and Formatting Graphic Objects

To move a graphic object, follow these steps:

1. Select the object; *handles* will appear around the object (see Figure 24-3).

2. Position the mouse pointer anywhere on the object.

3. Drag the object to the new position.

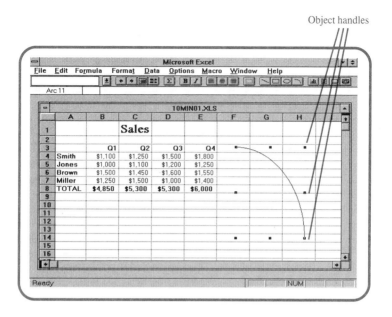

Figure 24-3. *An arc selected; note the handles around the object.*

To size a graphic object, follow these steps:

1. Select the object.

2. Grab one of the object handles.

3. Drag the handle until the object is the size or shape you want.

To format the border and fill pattern of a graphic object, follow these steps:

1. Select the object.

2. Pull down the Format menu.

3. Select the Patterns command.

115

4. Select the options. Note that if the graphic object is a line, a special dialog box appears (see Figure 24-4) that allows you to change line width and add arrowheads.

5. Click on OK or press Enter to close the dialog box. Excel automatically formats the selected object.

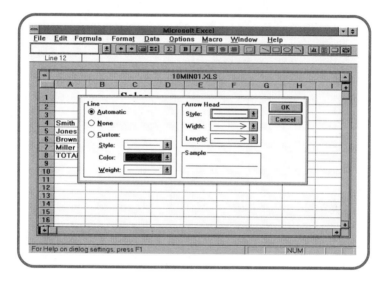

Figure 24-4. *The Format Patterns dialog box for a line.*

In this lesson you learned how to enhance your worksheets with text boxes and other graphic objects. In the next lesson you will learn how to put it all together and print your worksheet.

Lesson 25
Printing Excel Worksheets

In this lesson you'll learn how to print your worksheets.

Selecting the Print Area

If your worksheet is relatively simple, you can bypass the step of selecting the print area. Excel will automatically print any part of your worksheet that contains data or graphic objects. However, you may wish to customize the print area, especially if your worksheet flows across multiple pages.

To specify the area to print, follow these steps:

1. Highlight the range of cells you wish to print. If your worksheet contains a header you wish repeated from page to page, *do not select the header*.

2. Pull down the Options menu.

3. Select the Set Print Area option.

   Printing selected sections If you have a very large worksheet, you can use the Options Set Print Area command to print only selected areas of the worksheet.

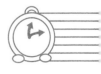

If you have a consistent header (such as a report title or column headings), you can have Excel automatically print these cells on each page by using the Options Set Print Titles command.

Follow these steps to assign print titles:

1. Select the rows for your print title (as shown in Figure 25-1.)

2. Pull down the Options menu.

3. Select the Set Print Titles option.

When your worksheet prints, the print title rows will appear on every page, above the selected print area.

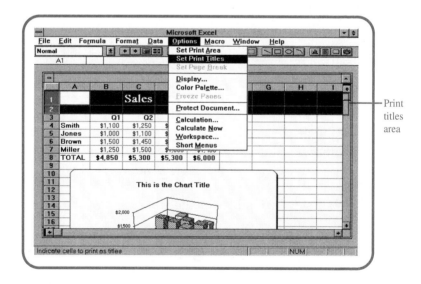

Figure 25-1. *Rows selected as print titles.*

Changing Print Settings

Before you print, you need to set up your page layout for printing. All relevent options are accessed with the File Page Setup command.

You can select from the following options:

Header/ Footer	Information typed in these boxes will appear as headers or footers on every page of your printout
Margins	Specifies the amount of space and the printed area of your worksheet
Center	Determines whether or not the document is centered vertically or horizontally on the page
Row & Column Headings	Determines whether or not row and column headings (A, B, C, etc.) are printed
Gridlines	Determines whether gridlines are printed

Printing Headings and Gridlines Most users turn off the Row & Column Headings and Gridlines options to produce a cleaner, more professional printed document.

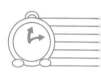

To set up the page layout settings, follow these steps:

1. Pull down the File menu.

2. Select the Page Setup option.

3. When the dialog box in Figure 25-2 appears, select the options.

4. Click on OK or press Enter to close the dialog box.

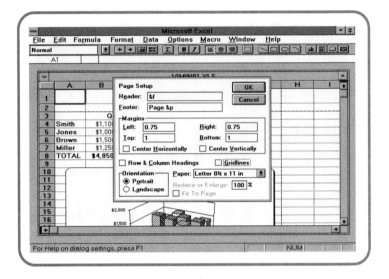

Figure 25-2. *The File Page Setup dialog box.*

Previewing Your Printout

After the page setup is completed, you can preview your printed document with the File Print Preview command. This command gives you a true WYSIWYG (What You See Is What You Get) preview.

To move to page preview, follow these steps:

1. Pull down the File menu.

2. Select the Print Preview option.

With this option engaged, Excel displays your document as it will look when printed (see Figure 25-3). While in the print preview screen, you can switch from page to page with the Next and Previous buttons; take a close-up view of the document with the Zoom button; display the page margins with the Margins button; alter the page setup with the Setup button; return to your on-screen worksheet with the Close button; and initiate printing with the Print button. You can also use the scroll bars to scroll through each page as previewed.

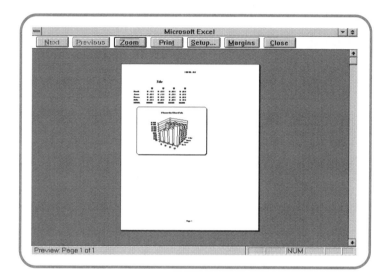

Figure 25-3. Excel's Print Preview screen.

Zooming in on the worksheet You can also zoom and unzoom the print preview by positioning the mouse pointer anywhere on the page preview display and clicking the left mouse button.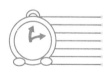

Printing the Worksheet

After you've set up the page and previewed the results, you can finally print your document. You can initiate printing directly from the print preview screen, or you can use the File Print command.

To print your document, follow these steps:

1. Pull down the File menu.

2. Select the Print option.

3. When the dialog box in Figure 25-4 appears, select the options.

4. Select OK to initiate printing.

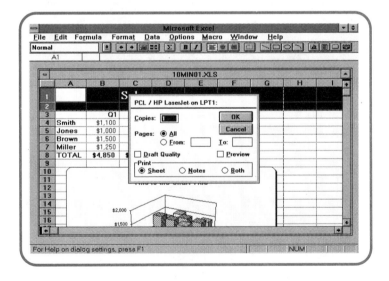

Figure 25-4. Selecting print options.

When areas don't print Make sure that all parts of the worksheet you want to print are selected. For example, to print a chart you have annotated into your worksheet, you must select the worksheet cells *under* the chart.

You've done it! Your worksheet is complete and printed. There is only one more operation we'll cover in this book: Command macros. Turn to the next lesson to learn how to automate some common Excel operations.

Lesson 26
Automating Your Work with Macros

In this lesson you'll learn how to create simple macros.

Macros let you automate repeated operations. Excel features a robust macro programming language, which you can use to create complex macros. You can also create simple macros by recording keystrokes and mouse movements. We will examine the latter method in this lesson.

Macro A macro is a set of instructions that tell Excel to perform specific tasks. When macros are run Excel performs the task automated by the macro.

Recording the Macro

To record a macro, follow these steps:

1. Pull down the Macro menu.

2. Select the Record command.

3. When the dialog box in Figure 26-1 appears, enter a descriptive name for the macro.

4. Enter a one-character shortcut key for the macro. When you play back the macro, this key—when activated simultaneously with the Ctrl key—will activate the macro.

5. Click on OK or press Enter to close the dialog box.

6. Perform any commands or actions you want to record in the macro. Excel will record your selections exactly.

7. When finished recording commands, pull down the Macro menu again.

8. Select the Stop Recorder option to turn off the macro recorder.

Your commands have now been recorded as a macro.

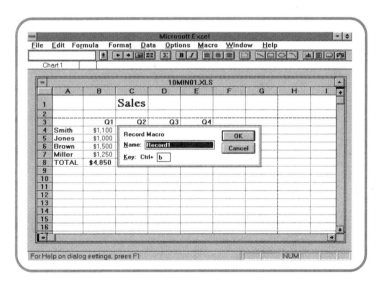

Figure 26-1. *The Macro Record dialog box.*

Uppercase and lowercase letters for shortcut keys Excel distinguishes between uppercase and lowercase letters in the Macro Record dialog box. Remember that typing *r* activates the lowercase r key, and typing *R* activates the uppercase R key. You must select your shortcut keys on a case-sensitive basis.

Excel actually writes macro programming codes for the macros you record. These codes are written in a separate macro file, which you must treat as you would a worksheet file. You can view the macro code by switching to the macro window (see Figure 26-2). You must also save the macro sheet, as well as open it when you want to apply it to a worksheet or group of worksheets.

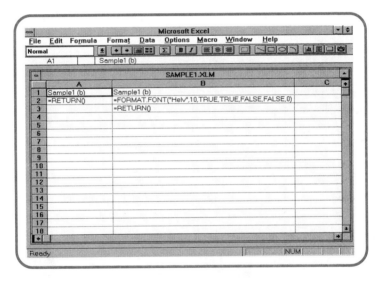

Figure 26-2. A sample macro sheet.

Opening macro sheets For efficient use, open all relevent macro sheets at the start of your work session. And remember to close your macro sheets at the end of the session.

Running the Macro

Once your macro has been recorded, you can run it at any time.

Saving macro sheets You must save your macro sheet—just like a worksheet—in order to preserve your macro. You must also have your macro sheet *open* to run the macro.

To run a macro, follow these steps:

1. Pull down the Macro menu.

2. Select the Run option.

3. Select the macro from the list displayed.

4. Choose OK to run the macro.

Using the shortcut key You can also run the macro using the shortcut key you specified when you recorded the macro. Simply press Ctrl and the shortcut key simultaneously.

Macros can be quite involved; some users program entire applications using macros. If you want to learn more about macros, consult one of the other SAMS books listed in the Introduction of this book.

With this lesson, you've completed the *10 Minute Guide to Excel for Windows*. Following this lesson is a list of useful Excel functions, as well as a brief Primer on essential DOS and Windows procedures. Remember, even though you've finished this book, keep it handy. These lessons are also useful as reminders when you can't recall how to perform specific tasks!

Appendix A
Table of Excel Worksheet Functions

Below is a list of the most common Excel built-in functions. The type of data to be used with the function is indicated in the parentheses.

Mathematical Functions

ABS(value)	Calculates the absolute value of a number
INT(value)	Rounds a number down to the nearest integer
MOD(dividend, divisor)	Calculates the modulus of a divisor and a dividend
PI( )	Used in the place of the value Pi
PRODUCT (value, value...)	Calculates the product of the specified values
ROUND (value, precision)	Rounds a value to a specified number of places

Statistical Functions

AVERAGE(range)	Calculates the mean average of a group of numbers
COUNT(range)	Counts the number of cells in a range that contain numeric values
COUNTA(range)	Counts the number of nonblank cells in a range
MIN(range)	Returns the minimum value in a range of cells
MAX(range)	Returns the maximum value in a range of cells
SUM(range)	Calculates the total of a group of cells

Financial Functions

DDB(cost, salvage, life, period, factor)	Calculates depreciation using the double declining balance method
FV(interest rate, periods, payment amount, present value, type)	Calculates the future value of an investment
IPMT(rate, period, periods, present value, future value, type)	Calculates the interest paid for a particular payment

NPER(rate, payment, present value, future value, type)	Calculates the number of payments required to pay off a loan at a given interest rate
NPV(rate, range)	Calculates the present value of a series of cash flow transactions
PMT(rate, periods, present value, future value, type)	Calculates the payment amount required for an investment to be paid off given a specific term and interest rate
PPMT(rate, period, periods, present value, future value, type)	Calculates the amount of principal being paid during any payment period
RATE(periods, payment, present value, future value, type, guess)	Calculates the interest rate required for a present value to become a greater value
SLN(cost, salvage, life)	Calculates depreciation using the straight line method
SYD(cost, salvage, life, period)	Calculates depreciation using the sum of the years' digits method

Logical Functions

IF(condition, value if true, value if false)	Tests whether a condition is true or false

ISBLANK(cell)	Tests whether a cell is blank
ISERR(cell)	Tests whether a cell contains an error

Date\Time Functions

DATEVALUE(text)	Converts a text string into a valid date
DAY(date)	Returns the day corresponding to a specified date
MONTH(date)	Returns the month corresponding to a specified date
NOW( )	Returns the current date and time, using the DOS startup date and time
TIMEVALUE(text)	Converts a text string into a valid time
WEEKDAY(date)	Returns the weekday name of any valid date
YEAR(date)	Returns the year corresponding to a specified date

DOS and Windows Primer

This section highlights some of the DOS and Windows procedures you will use during your work with this program.

DOS is your computer's Disk Operating System. It functions as a go-between program that lets the various components of your computer system talk with one another. Whenever you type anything using your keyboard, whenever you move your mouse, whenever you print a file, DOS interprets the commands and coordinates the task.

Windows is an operating environment that works with DOS. Windows sits *on top* of DOS and provides a user-friendly interface to some of DOS' more complicated procedures. Just as DOS functions as a go-between for the components of your computer system, Windows functions as a go-between for you and your computer.

The following sections explain how to run some essential DOS functions on your computer, as well as how to use Windows to perform more advanced tasks.

Using DOS

If you are running Windows, your computer has a hard disk. DOS is probably already installed on your hard disk, which means that when you turn on your computer, DOS automatically loads itself without any special installation. (Some computer manufacturers configure their computers so that Windows also automatically loads when you turn on your PC. If this is the case, you might want to skip the next section.)

Once DOS is loaded, you should see a *prompt* (known as the DOS prompt) on your screen that looks something like **C:** or **C:>**. This prompt tells you which disk drive is currently active; most hard drives are labeled as drive C. The floppy disk drives located on the front of your computer are drives A and B. If you only have one floppy drive, it's usually the A drive. If you have two floppy drives, the top or left drive is usually A, and the bottom or right drive is B.

You can change to a different drive at any time by following these steps:

1. If you're changing to a floppy drive, make sure that there is a formatted disk in that drive.

2. Type the letter of the drive you wish to change to, followed by a colon. For example, type **a:**.

3. Press Enter. The DOS prompt changes to show that the drive you selected is now the active drive.

Managing Directories and Files in DOS

Because hard disks hold much more information than floppy disks, hard disks are often divided into smaller parts, called *directories*. Each directory is like a branch off the main tree trunk; in the computer world, the main tree trunk is called the *root* directory. Each directory branching from the root directory can branch out to other *subdirectories*; each subdirectory can also have branching subdirectories, and so on. Note that each directory and subdirectory has a unique name that allows you to access that directory from DOS or Windows.

Making Directories in DOS

To create a new directory use the DOS Make Directory command. This command is invoked when you type **md**, followed by the name of the new directory (including the complete path). For example, to create a directory called NEW, you would type

md c:\new

If you wanted to create a subdirectory called NEW-A as a branch from the NEW directory, you would type

md c:\new\new-a

Changing Directories in DOS

To change to a different directory, use the Change Directory command. This command is invoked when you type **cd**, followed by a backslash (\) and the name of the directory you wish to change to. For example, to move to the NEW directory, you would type

135

cd\new

If you wanted to move to the NEW-A subdirectory that branches from the NEW directory, you would type the complete *path* in the Change Directory command, as follows:

cd\new\new-a

Listing Files with DOS

To display files within a directory, use the DOS Directory command. Follow these steps:

1. Use the CD command to change to the directory.

2. Type **DIR**.

3. Press Enter.

   DOS displays a list of files in this directory.

Copying Files with DOS

The DOS Copy command copies the selected file to a second location, either on your hard disk or on a floppy disk. Follow these steps to copy a file:

1. Use the CD command to move to the directory that contains the source file.

2. Type the command line

   COPY filename1 filename2

Filename1 is your original file; filename2 is the new file. You can also specify a new path for the target file, using the syntax **[drive]:\[path]\filename2**.

3. Press Enter.

DOS then copies the file.

Deleting Files with DOS

DOS uses the Erase command to delete files from your disks. To delete a file, follow these steps:

1. Use the CD command to move to the directory.

2. Type the command line

   ERASE filename

3. Press Enter.

4. When DOS asks for confirmation, type **Y**.

   DOS then deletes the file.

Using DISKCOPY to Make Backups of the Excel Program Disks

Before you install Excel on your hard disk, you should make *backup copies* of the original program disks. By using these backup copies to install the program, you avoid the risk of damaging the original disks.

Obtain 3 blank 5.25" double-sided double-density disks or 2 blank 3.5" double-sided double-density disks. The type of disk should be marked on the package. Because the DISKCOPY command copies the entire disk, you don't have to format the disks before you begin.

To copy your program disks, use the DOS Diskcopy command. This command differs from the normal Copy command in that it copies the contents of an entire disk. Follow these steps:

1. Since DOS program files are normally located on your hard disk, change to drive C by typing **c:** and then pressing Enter.

2. If the DISKCOPY file is in a separate directory, change to that directory by typing **cd\(name of directory)**. For example, if the file is in the C:\DOS directory, type **cd\dos** at the C: prompt, and press Enter.

3. Type **diskcopy a: a:** or **diskcopy b: b:**, depending on which drive you're using to make the copies, then press Enter. A message appears, telling you to insert the source diskette into the floppy drive.

4. Insert the original Excel disk you want to copy (the *source* disk) into drive A (or B) and press Enter. DOS copies the disk into memory, then sends an on-screen message telling you to insert the *target* diskette (one of your blank disks) into the floppy drive.

5. Insert one of your blank disks into the floppy drive and press Enter. DOS copies the disk from memory onto the blank disk. When the copying is complete, a message appears asking if you want to copy another diskette.

6. Remove the disk from the drive and label it with the same name and number that appears on the original disk.

7. Repeat this procedure for all the original Excel disks; remember to press Y when DOS asks you if you want to copy another disk.

8. When you have finished copying the last disk, answer N when DOS asks you if you want to copy another disk. Remember to put the original disks back into their box and to store them in a safe place.

Basic Windows Procedures

Windows is a Graphical User Interface (GUI) for DOS-based computers. Many users consider the Windows screen (interface) *friendlier* than the DOS prompt. Windows includes a program called the File Manager that allows you to work with disks, directories, and files.

To properly use Windows, however, you have to master some techniques that might be unfamiliar to a typical DOS user.

Starting Windows

To start Windows, follow these steps:

1. Change to the drive that contains your Windows files, usually drive C:.

2. Change to the directory that contains your Windows files, usually C:\WINDOWS, by typing cd\windows.

3. Type WIN and press Enter. DOS will automatically start Windows.

Using the Mouse

One Windows procedure that might be new to a DOS user is the use of the *mouse*. Mastering the mouse is essential to effective Windows performance.

You need to master the following techniques to use the mouse with Windows:

Point   Move the mouse pointer to an item on-screen

Click   Press and release the mouse button once (quickly); often used to high-light an item in Windows

Double-click   Press and release the mouse button twice (quickly); often used to select an item in Windows

Drag   Press the mouse button and hold it down while you move the mouse; this enables you to grab an on-screen object and move it across the screen

While the mouse is recommended for most efficient Windows use, you can use the keyboard for many of the same operations. In many cases Windows and Windows applications let you use special function key and combination key shortcuts to quickly access menu items and commands via the keyboard. The inside back cover of this book lists some common keyboard shortcuts for Excel.

Managing Directories and Files with the Windows File Manager

Windows includes a special program called the File Manager. The File Manager automates many of the tasks traditionally implemented by DOS commands, including functions for working with directories, formatting disks, and listing, copying, and deleting files. Most users find it easier to work with the icons and menus of the Windows File Manager than trying to remember the exact syntax needed to use traditional DOS commands.

The File Manager is opened by double-clicking on the File Manager icon in the Main Program Group.

Making Directories with the File Manager

The File Manager displays both a visual representation of your directory tree and a list of individual files in each directory. When the File Manager first starts, you are shown a tree with all the main directories branching off from the root directory of your current disk drive. You can change drives displayed by clicking on the appropriate drive icon.

To make a new directory, follow these steps:

1. Pull down the File menu.

2. Select the Create Directory option.

3. Type the path and name of the new directory in the dialog box.

4. Close the dialog box by double-clicking on the OK button or by pressing Enter.

Changing Directories with the File Manager

The File Manager displays a tree listing all directories branching off from the root directory. You can display subdirectories by clicking on any directory icon that shows a plus (+) sign.

You can make any directory or subdirectory active by moving the mouse pointer to the directory name and clicking the mouse button. The active directory name is now highlighted.

Listing Files with the File Manager

To display the contents of any directory, follow these steps:

1. Highlight the appropriate directory or subdirectory.

2. Double-click on the directory icon.

Windows displays a *directory window* that lists all the files in the selected directory. You can display multiple directory windows on-screen simultaneously.

Copying Files with the File Manager

Copying files from one directory to another or from one disk to another is easy with Windows. To copy a file, follow these steps:

1. Select the file to copy in the directory window by placing the mouse pointer over the file name and clicking the mouse button. The file name is now highlighted.

2. To copy the file to another directory, click and hold the left mouse button over the highlighted file, and then drag the file out of the directory window to the appropriate directory in the directory tree. (When you drag the file, the mouse pointer changes to a small file icon.)

3. With the mouse pointer positioned over the target directory, release the mouse button to *drop* the copy of the file into the directory.

You can also copy the file to another disk by dropping the file icon onto one of the drive icons at the top of the directory file window. Make sure that if the target drive is a floppy drive, it contains a formatted floppy disk.

Deleting Files with the File Manager

To delete a file with the File Manager, follow these steps:

1. Select the file to delete in the directory window.

2. Pull down the File menu.

3. Click on the Delete option.

4. When the dialog box appears, click on the Delete button to delete the highlighted file, or on the Cancel button to cancel the delete operation.

More Information on DOS and Windows

This section presented essential information on DOS and Windows operations. For more detailed instruction, consult the following SAMS books:

10 Minute Guide to MS-DOS

10 Minute Guide to Windows 3

First Book of MS-DOS

Best Book of MS-DOS

First Book of Excel 3 for Windows

Index